Meetings with Spiritual Masters

A Memoir

By Charles Paprocki

Carbondale, IL
November, 2020

Copyright 2020 by Chuck Paprocki

All rights reserved under International and Pan-American Copyright Conventions

Published in the United States by
Inner World Publications
P.O. Box 1613, San German, Puerto Rico, 00683

Library of Congress Control Number:
2020952875

ISBN:
978188171829

All rights reserved. This book, or parts thereof, may not be reproduced in any form or by any means, electronic or mechanical, including photocopying, recording, or by any information storage or retrieval system, without the permission of the publisher except for brief quotations.

Cover print provided by Tina Ullrich-Furness, an artist with a BFA in sculpture and a doctorate in clinical psychology. In the last three decades most of her work has centered on Portraiture and Mandala-Making. More of her work can be seen at: ullrich-mandalas.com.

Contents

Part One: Miracle On 47th Street 5

Part Two: The Wave Of Love 29

Part Three: Inside Me, Outside Me 59

Part Four: A Matter Of Style 147

Part One

Miracle On 47th Street

Introduction

A teacher I had in high school once told my class that every human being's life is unique and we could all learn something important from anybody if we ever took the time. I don't recall what prompted him to say this, but this little idea, uttered in an off-handed way, stuck with me throughout my life, like some things mysteriously tend to do. Now at fifty-six years old, I'm sitting in a Starbuck's on Fifth Avenue and 33rd Street in Manhattan looking at the army of worker bees trudging to their office buildings in the rain and this little thought flutters through my mind again.

I am a nobody. But my life, as the little saying goes, has been unique. And looking about me I know that everyone out there walking in the rain has also led a unique life. Would I dare "take the time" to walk up to a table, introduce myself, and sit down to share a story with a stranger? Nope. I'm a normal guy. In a place like New York City, there are too many people. Actually, we don't really see each other as people like that. We're more like creatures who look somewhat like each other, but we do different things and play different roles. For example, that guy serving the coffee. He's not a human being; he's the counter clerk. If he engaged me as a human being for more than a sentence or two, I'd get irritated and have to cut him off. That guy reading the newspaper in his black suit, he's a broker. If I need a broker I'll talk to him in his place of business. If not, I won't talk to him. This approach simplifies things and allows us to keep our sanity. If we meet someone in a social setting, the first thing we've got to know is what the other person does for work. In a modern society like this, everyone has to make things and buy things. These are the ground rules of human interaction. If you don't do these things, then people will look right passed you.

They will ask you just once, what do you do and if you don't have a good answer, you've just lost your human status. They'll let you rot to death just outside the door of Starbucks.

You can't really blame people for this. In our evolution, we've always needed stuff to stay alive and we always wanted more stuff just for fun. Now we've got that. In some ways, New York is heaven. If you're already in heaven and you don't want to hear any more of my rambling, then I tip my hat to you. Cruise on.

If anybody is still reading, then here's the thing. The uniqueness of my personal life stems from the idea that as human beings, we have an existential value that underlies our utility value and that it is from the exploration of one's existential value that real magic occurs in life. If you've seen pictures of the beatified saints, Christ walking on water and raising the dead, the blue baby Krishna, the Tibetan demons, yogis in caves, bilocation, precognition, Yoda, the doctor who sticks his hand in your stomach and pulls out your disease, bliss, joy, hellish nightmares, sucking at the devil's asshole. That's what I'm talking about. I can tell you something about these things. Granted, I can't tell you a lot because I'm a family man and have had to do all the same things that you do to keep the family alive, but I can tell you some magical things if you want to hear them.

Alright then. For starters, you can't tell much by looking at me. I'm as average as an American can be. Born and bred in a Chicago suburb with every house on the block a look-a-like and every strip mall with its MacDonald's and Midas Mufflers. I'm middle class. (Probably lower middle class.) I've got a college degree in English from a little Catholic College outside Chicago. I went to graduate school in Southern Illinois, but the whole thing made me sick, so I became a Hippy and planned Earth Day and got involved in other things like that. I'm not a Hippy anymore, but back then it was average to be a Hippy. There is no single experience to which I can attribute the start of my journey along the path less traveled by, but as far back as I can remember, my parents went to church and I could never figure out why.

What I am about to share with you is ninety-nine percent true. I took a little poetic license here or there to protect the innocent, but this is a story of how magic happens to someone like me who ventures down the path less traveled by. While most people experience God through signs and symbolic events in their lives, occasionally, although rare, some people have the experience of meeting God in a human body. When God is in a human body, we call such a person a Spiritual Master. This is my story of meeting three such men.

Subconsciousness

The creek bed leading down to Little Grand Canyon is dry now, the rocks and boulders covered with flakes of lichen glow pale blue-green and mustard in the dim light. A dense canopy of tree branches blots out the sky but for tiny brilliant shafts of light that break the thick hypnosis of the forest floor.

The air is sticky and hot. Mosquitoes whine in my ear and flit in my hair as I make my way down the creek bed. A dragon fly appears from nowhere; its iridescent blue body hovers motionless for a moment before my eyes, and then quickly darts away.

With every inhalation I smell the perfume of new life mixed with the mold of decay; it's intense like the musk of a large animal. A black crow caws mournfully to warn others that I am coming. Small birds tweet high overhead.

Leaping on to a boulder, I stand there to catch my breath and look into the view finder of my camera. I point it down the creek bed but the red light warns me that it is too dark to take a picture.

"So that's that!" I feel a curious sense of liberation. I am no longer responsible for taking pictures to show my family and friends back in New York. I am alone now in the Shawnee forest of southern Illinois and from now on what I see belongs only to me.

I immediately become suspicious that God may test me now. Before I can respond to this feeling, I look down to see a lime-green snake, thick as a half dollar and two-feet in length, slither off the rock by my foot and enter a shadowy patch of weeds along the bank.

I remember someone telling me that bobcats, coyotes, and panthers have returned to southern Illinois to hunt the growing deer population and I forget the snake and look deeply into the dark forest that surrounds me.

I continue down the creek bed until I come upon a fallen maple tree. The tree has been there a long time . . . years, considering how the bark has been stripped by the running water and the huge trunk has settled now, no more than two or three feet from the stones in the creek bed, sagging more each year as its limbs rot and break off. Large logs, brush, and debris carried by the water are wedged up against the trunk making it impossible for me to duck under the tree. I have to go around or over. To my left, a large cake of dirt and clay still hangs from the tree's upturned roots and creates an imposing wall at least ten feet high. Brambles and brush grow all around the base of the wall and extend out along the creek bed. On the other bank, the crown of the tree forms an impenetrable network of large branches covered with vines and protruding stakes of smaller trees that had been crushed or cracked by the maple when it fell. I can also see poison ivy running up along the bank.

I wipe the sweat from my eyebrows and begin to climb over the dead wood and branches to get up on the trunk. I narrowly miss plunging my foot into a slimy hole of water hidden near the base of the trunk but manage to get up okay. Standing on the trunk and looking down, my head is about twelve feet above the rocks on the creek bed. I test my balance on the smooth trunk. I find a branch of dead wood that was not yet rotten and snap it off to serve as a walking stick or, if need be, a weapon.

It occurs to me then in an intuitive flash that I will have to fight a demon. A demon? Did I mean a bobcat? A snake? A wild dog? My mind scans the feeling. No . . . No . . . No . . . it said a demon.

An icy logic works through the network of my brain cells: I had been on the path to God for many years. I had been there when the veil of reality had been rent and God exposed his beautiful face to me. I had looked into the beauty and mystery of that face with my own eyes until I could no longer stand it and collapsed in a swirling bliss. When such a thing happens to a person, the hold that material reality has on the mind gets loosened. It's as if once you've seen a woman naked you are less enamored by the clothing she wears no matter how seductive it may be.

I realize the awful truth that once a devotee of God penetrates the illusion of physical forms, that God will send even more powerful pleasures and evils to grab his attention and divert his mind from wanting God. Its how the game of self-realization works. Do you love me for me or do you just love my body.

I understand now too well the meaning behind the Tibetan demons and the awful masks of God that primitive people have made. The demons will come to test my constancy, my love, and my faith in God so that I may plumb the depth of my attachments. And, yes, they will also come in order for God to know the truth about me as well. In this way, it does not matter wherein the demon arises, either from the depths of my own mind or from the will of God, it matters not.

"Do you believe that I love you and that I will protect you against all evil?"

"Yes, my Lord."

"And you say that you love me more than life itself and you will undergo any trial to prove your love for me."

"Yes, Father."

"Then, so be it, my precious boy."

A strong wind rushes up from the valley floor and batters my clothing. "So fucking be it!!!" I scream at the top of my lungs. Adrenaline gushes in my veins and my head feels like it will split open from the pain. The sky rotates wildly overhead and the forest swirls around me. Suddenly, it all becomes very quiet and dreamlike and I can see the demon standing down the creek bed, naked, covered in red slime.

I have lost my civilization now and stand sniffing and grunting like a hominid. I can smell the Death Goddess again in this place. Sweaty, hot, whiney, and rotten.

She has sent one of her living-dead to slay me. I am scared shitless. I brush the scalding sweat from my eyes and run screaming at him. He does not move as I charge frantically at him. When I am close enough I lunge at him swinging my stick wildly above my head. With deftness, he steps aside and I trip awkwardly on my face. Now, standing over me transformed into a giant green snake, he spits poison in my face that smells of mother's milk. I scramble wildly for my stick but it is too late. The poison has taken affect. I find myself falling down a black bottomless pit. I fall for hours, days, until I no longer know I'm falling. I don't know if I am awake or asleep. I don't know anything.

Self-Consciousness

My mother and father had met in the army toward the end of World War II and soon after this meeting my mother became pregnant with me. She was brought up in a coal miner's family on the outskirts of Mascoutah Illinois, with two sisters, an outhouse in the backyard, and a farm across the road where she went each morning to buy milk and eggs. My father's family mostly worked for Western Electric and Mary Queen of Heaven, a Catholic parish in Cicero, Illinois, a working class suburb just west of Chicago. Both families were good Catholics. They went to mass on Sunday, went to confession regularly, and upheld the sacraments.

When my parents were discharged from the army, they had little money and housing was hard to come by. A lot of soldiers were being discharged toward the end of the war in the same situation. My family, which now included my brother Tom, one year younger than me, moved into a barracks town that the government threw up in a large field that bordered an upper middle-class neighborhood on the south side of Chicago.

Each unit had two apartments in it. Our unit was the first home I remember. The roof was tin and leaked when it rained. A storage shed stood beside the front door. When you looked out the front door you could see about six other barracks. The road in and out of the barracks town was gravel. One of my first memories is the glare of the sun on the windows of the passing cars and the cloud of dust when they passed.

My parents have a picture of me in a play pen in front of the barracks. I'm standing and holding the bars with a serious face and knitted brows. When my parent's friends came to visit, they'd drink beer and pass me around trying to get me to smile. I'm told I was a big source of amusement to everyone because I rarely did.

I was born white. This puts me on the top of the color scheme according to the values of the ruling class. However, I'm on the low end of the white scale because I am Slavic.

I got my first taste of racism, like a guzzle of sour milk, when I was five years old. I guess it was one of those triggers that started me on my quest to discover what it meant to be a human being.

One day about dinnertime, we heard a large commotion out on the road. People were milling around and talking loudly. Men swore and shook their arms at the sky. I walked outside with dad, while mom stood in the doorway with Tommy.

Somebody shouted, "The niggers are coming." People were edgy. A woman started to cry hysterically. I could feel the fear and anger of the people and became petrified. "Niggers? What are niggers?" I thought. I imagined an unspeakable horde of demons with long sharp teeth that ate people.

The crowd grew. They mostly had their backs to us, looking down the road away from our house. Some men had baseball bats, but I knew they weren't going to play baseball with the niggers. Suddenly we heard sirens and a lot of police showed up and made everyone go back to their houses. People continued to grumble. "Fuck the niggers," I heard one man spit.

The next day Tommy and I were playing out on the gravel road with Jessie and Tyrone. We were loading our toy dump trucks with the small rocks. We liked Jesse and Tyrone better than Billy Thompson who lived in the apartment on the other side of us, and better than Mickey Sullivan whose dad was pals with our dad.

Still thinking about last night, I ask Jessie and Tyrone in a solemn tone if they heard that the niggers were coming. They shake their heads no, but I can tell they know what I'm talking about. "What's a nigger?" Jesse asks. I hunch my shoulders. In the silence that follows we are united in the recognition that the world is full of scary things we don't know about.

After a while, I tell Jesse and Tyrone that Tommy and I want to go to the park and play. I ask them if they want to come. They say yes. The park is a beautiful place with soft grass, swings, slides, tennis courts, baseball fields, water fountains, and ice cream stands. We trek across the stretch of barren dirt and weeds that separates our barracks town from the tall trees and high wrought iron fence that runs along the perimeter of the park.

At the gate there is a guardhouse. When we reach the gate, the guard comes out. He seems like a nice man and Tom and I had always said "Hi" when we passed him. This time he stops Jesse and Tyrone who are walking behind us. I turn around and look at him. He says to me:

"You boys can go ahead but there's no nigger boys allowed."

"Nigger boys?!" What does he mean? I get scared. What does he know that we don't know? I know Jessie and Tyrone, they're good guys. "They're not nigger boys, they're our friends," I yell.

"Call 'em what you want. They can't go in."

Righteous indignation overwhelms me. The guard stands there with one hand on Jesse's head and the other on Tyrone's and he won't let them go into the park because he thinks they're niggers. I can't fathom it. How can he not see the difference between my friends who are little boys and niggers who are monsters? And he's a grownup!

With blind fury, I scream at the guard at the top of my lungs that he's a "Jerk" and Tommy calls him an "Ass" which makes us all laugh and we run back to the safety of barracks town. None of us knew what to make of it, so we went and got our cowboy guns and forgot the whole thing. But of course we never did forget it.

When I was six years old, my parents moved into a two-story house that my aunts Eleanor and Irene owned in Cicero. Both of them worked as housekeepers in the Mary Queen of

Heaven rectory two blocks away and they were strict. They made innuendoes about Tommy's and my behavior and the fact that our mom was too lenient with us. Of course, I had to admit Tommy was a wild kid. Sometimes, they would invite Tommy and me to go upstairs to their apartment and eat pie and drink chocolate milk. We'd always steal a couple of marbles from their fish tank before we left.

Cicero was an all-white town that bordered a large black ghetto on Chicago's west side. The ghetto was growing very fast as Blacks were uprooted from southern farms during the post war industrialization process that replaced the need for human labor with tractors.

Cicero was mainly second and third generation Italians, Poles, Bohemians, and Lithuanians who lived in the older two-story, wood frame houses or the newer, squat, brick bungalows. The men worked in the local factories. The white people were scared that a black person would move into Cicero and reduce their property values. Every now and then you'd hear about a black family that moved across Cicero Avenue into Cicero and got their home burned down for their effort. It wouldn't be an arsonist in the dead of night. It was always a mob of angry people, mostly young men, who would gather after dinner to make taunts and throw rocks at the house. Then someone would light a fire and they'd watch the building burn down as it got dark. After hearing about this a few times, I could discern a pattern in life. White people being on the lookout that the niggers were coming.

In Cicero, I went to Mary Queen of Heaven school. Nuns taught me to pray to God so that he would help stop the evil in the world. We learned that only Catholics could enter heaven. And if there was one thing that could keep a Catholic out of heaven, it was sex. But that vital bit of information came later around sixth grade.

By second grade, I recognized two big divisions between people. White people and Black people and Catholics and Protestants. It was a mortal sin to go to a Protestant church, even to walk up the steps and look in the door. There was a Protestant church on the corner of my block but I didn't know anyone who went there. I wasn't scared of Protestants though.

I couldn't say the same about Black people. I was scared of them. I didn't know any Blacks in Cicero because there weren't any, but I knew they were different. I associated them with the six o'clock news and police drawings of criminals that were hung on the bulletin board in the post office. Blacks liked knives. They walked around in gangs. They didn't talk like me. They took drugs. I also knew that they stayed on one side of Cicero Avenue and we stayed on the other.

Growing up in Cicero I got in my share of fistfights. I gained a reputation after beating up the biggest kid in my class in a fight at the Boys Club. Kids also knew that if somebody attacked Tommy or me they would have to fight the other as well. My dad had put up a punching bag in our basement and Tommy and I used to hit it every day. We also beat the shit out of each other for fun.

My dad always wanted to be a journalist and actually started college before the war, but when he got out of the army he was married and had to get a job. He had different kinds of truck routes as we were growing up. First, it was a laundry route, then a milk route with Bowman dairy, then a route with a company called Chili-O that sold frozen hamburger patties and five pound bricks of frozen chili to restaurants and diners in the city.

He and mom had bigger ambitions for us kids than to work in the factories. When Tommy and I outgrew Mary Queen of Heaven, they sent us to St Procopius Academy in Lisle, Illinois. This was my dad's old school. It was run by Benedictine monks. It was okay. It was a big mix of kids from different suburbs, but also included some tough neighborhoods in Chicago and richer neighborhoods out in the western suburbs. In our freshman and sophomore years we got in a lot of fights to prove ourselves and get things all lined out.

God-Consciousness

When I was a junior my parents moved to Westmont, Illinois, which had bigger trees, greener grass, and was more middle class. During summer break that year, I got my first job at a place called Follett's, a used textbook business that bought, rebound, and resold books. It operated from a five-story warehouse on the west side of Chicago. At Follett's, I worked with two large black men named Charles Little and Leroy Short. They were both great storytellers. They were also Pentecostal ministers in the same church. They said their church was in an old theatre on 47th Street on the south side. I immediately liked both of them, especially Charles.

Leroy sang opera to himself as he went about his business of stocking newly rebound books in the long rows of metal bins that took up most of the floor. He had a beautiful baritone voice and always had a flashy smile for me. He'd catch me out of the corner of his eye and come over to talk to me, keeping one eye out for the bosses. He'd speak in a hushed voice and tell me that I was wasting my life drinking wine and chasing girls when God could fill me with joy forever. This stuff would just roll out of his mouth. I'd tell him to go to hell and he'd just laugh and keep talking his shtick. The thing was I never felt judged or put down. It was more like a joke between us. Leroy told me that he found God when he fell into a lake of "night soil" behind a village while patrolling during the Korean War. After hearing the story a couple of times I realized that night soil was human shit. I guessed that I would call out to God too if I was drowning in shit.

Although Leroy was around, stacking books in the bins, I worked more closely with Charles. We unpacked boxes of used books and sorted them according to title and wear and tear, then put the books on pallets to be stocked or taken downstairs for rebinding. Charles also made it his business to educate me about God. But first he told me about himself. He said he was once a junky, a thief, a drunkard, and a bad man. One day he reached the end of his rope pissing blood in a phone booth. Witnessing the depths to which he had fallen on that fateful day, Charles begged God for forgiveness and offered a pact. As many men had done before, he promised that if God would save his life, Charles would dedicate himself to God's work. Remarkably, God obliged.

He spoke to Charles that day making it clear that having a relationship with Him was not just a one way street with the sinner doing all the talking. God said, "Charles, look what you've done to yourself. Pull yourself together now, I need you for my work." God then showed Charles his entire miserable life in minute details, which Charles's bugged out brain could never have recalled on its own. God told him that despite his miserable existence he was still his blessed son.

Charles couldn't believe that God loved him so much, because he was a man who nobody trusted, a man whose teeth were stained blue-black from tobacco and the wine, a man that would just as soon cut you as look at you. The experience in the phone booth turned Charles's life around. He quit smoking and drinking, got a job, and saved enough money to go to Moody Bible School and become a preacher.

By the time I met Charles, he was the happiest man I had ever met. Not stupid happy. He had a range of emotions, but under it all, he was definitely filled with honest to God joy. When I tried to articulate this to him one day, he laughed and called it the Holy Ghost.

Charles was built like Leroy, big with a broad chest and his hair cut close to the scalp. He came to work each day in a clean, white tee shirt and gray work pants. He always smelled of baby powder.

Although I loved Charles he wasn't very educated and I secretly felt superior to him. We'd actually have arguments about whether the world was flat or not. Charles believed it was flat because the bible referred to "the four corners of the earth". Once I brought a picture of the planet taken from a satellite to show him. He brushed it aside with a sour face. He told me the media made it up. "Chuck, you can't believe what you see in this world. You can only believe God."

I looked at him like he's full of shit. In response, he pretends he's looking at a TV set. "Here comes the Lone Ranger. He's riding through the pass on his horse Silver. 'Hi Ho Silver.' Oh, what's that . . . Look out! There's Pecos Slim on that boulder. Slim jumps on the Lone Ranger. They fly through the air and hit the ground. They smack each other end over end. Pop. Pop. Pop. They fall off a cliff into a lake. Slim holds the Lone Ranger's head under water. The Lone Ranger flips Slim and gets on top of him. Pop Pop. Finally Slim's had enough. "Stop Lone Ranger, you win." The Lone Ranger pulls him to the shore and holds his gun on him. And you know what Chuck. You notice anything strange about this?

"What's that?"

"They still both got their hats on!?" Charles bursts out laughing. "You don't think that's a lie!?"

He goes back to sorting books, chuckling to himself, knowing he beat me.

I know there's no sense arguing with Charles. It doesn't even matter. Charles may not have it all figured out reality wise, but he's got something going on. And you know what, I'm thinking, it could be worth the trade. He can burst out in song at any moment to praise

Jesus and the light in his face and the love in his heart is the real thing. I want to be with Charles as much as I can because he makes me laugh and feel good. I am like a son to him in a strange way.

I worked a couple summers with Charles before I entered college and then it looked like that was that. Our worlds weren't likely to cross again. But during my freshman year a tragedy struck my family and out of desperation, I sought Charles out. I believed that he was the only man on earth who could make things right.

My mother had just given birth to my youngest brother, Dave. We had a big Catholic family. There was me, Tom, Jim, Judy, Steve, Jane, Gary and now Dave. I was nineteen years old. It should have been a happy time, but my father came back from the hospital that night and told us that my mother had a viral infection that had dangerously enlarged her heart. She would not be coming home from the hospital. Choking back his tears, he said that she would not live long and would be an invalid until she died.

We could not accept this. It was a night of wailing and gnashing of teeth. It was our worst nightmare come to life. How could this happen. How do nightmares materialize like this?

"But who will take care of us?" Steve who was eight wanted to know.

"We're too little to see mommy in the hospital," Janey cried. Janey was four and she thought that she would never see our mother again.

My dad calmed the little kids down by saying that she "might" be able to come home sometime, but even if she did, he cautioned, she would be in a wheel chair and would not be able to take care of us. I had this image of our family like bowling pins standing together one second and then a ball comes crashing through and blows the family apart. My mother's sister, aunt Kate came up from Mascoutah the next day and stayed with us. After a couple of weeks she took baby Dave and the two youngest, Gary and Jane, with her back to Mascoutah.

My Dad would come home from the Chili-O route beat to shit, his face the pallor of rotten meat. Tommy and I would put a bowl of Campbell Soup and some Wonder Bread in front of him. We were at our wits end. No mother, our family split apart, and my dad barely making it. I never prayed so much in my life but it didn't seem to do any good. I kept thinking about Charles. I thought if anyone could help my mother he could. I knew that he loved God and God must love him. Charles had even told me about people getting cured at his church services.

Yet, for a couple of reasons I resisted going to see Charles. First, I would have to go into the black ghetto in Chicago and I didn't know how to get there and if I did go, would I get out alive. From what I remembered Charles saying, their prayer meeting was on Friday night—pay day, when the city was the wildest and out of control. Second, and more disturbing, what if Charles didn't heal my mother? I couldn't bare losing my mother, and losing faith in God on top of it.

There was also something else burrowing like a mole in my brain that I didn't want to even admit to myself. But one night in bed I went down in there and shook it out. It was this. What if Charles cured my mother? Wouldn't I then have to become a member of his church, out of principle? Out of doing the right thing? If God was in Charles' church stronger than he was in the Catholic Church in Westmont, wouldn't I have to acknowledge this and be true to my attempt to know God? If Charles cured my mother, how could I remain a Catholic anymore? The thought of being the only white boy going to a store front church on 47th Street every Friday night made me really, really uneasy. Charles had made a point of telling me there was a young Jewish man who came to his church, but I didn't know any Jews at that time and this made me feel even more squeamish. I tossed and turned with these problems each night for over a week, but eventually the sense of dread of my mother's death overcame all other feelings.

If I was to go to south Chicago I would need backup. I asked the guys from the street corner in Cicero who I grew up with if they would go with me. They all liked my mother and were willing to do it. When Friday night came, we loaded up the trunk full of baseball bats and twelve of us piled into two cars and headed down the Eisenhower expressway to Chicago.

We eventually found 47th Street on the Southside and after cruising up and down several times, we spotted what we thought might be Charles and Leroy's Pentecostal Church. The street was packed with people. Bars, diners, restaurants, and merchandise stores were all lit up. It was a cold Friday night in March. We parked our cars on a side street and got out slowly and stood around for a couple of minutes checking out the scene. We were nervous as hell and the looks that people gave us didn't help. They were as scared as we were. Frank unlocked the trunk and was standing by it just in case. We didn't know if it was the right church and if it wasn't what would we do then. Should we take the bats with us? I voted the idea down.

We were in our typical Cicero street corner clothes. Some of us wore gray work pants, white tee shirts and black construction boots. Others, me included, were more dressed up. We wore our iridescent shark skin pants and pointy-toed Italian shoes. We all wore black leather jackets. Not the kind with all that silver button shit. The kind that is cut like a suit coat and looks good. We swung around the corner onto 47th Street en masse walking fast toward the Church. People got out of our way, but stood and stared at our backs. A couple of cars slowed down to look. After about a half a block, we could hear singing coming from the open doors of the church. As we stomped into the lobby we were stopped by three panicky ushers in dark suits.

Through a doorway I could see Charles on the stage and a church full of people. I breathed a deep sigh of relief. I told the usher we were here to see Brother Charles. He looked incredulous. I managed to inch over to the doorway and wave to Charles. He immediately stopped his preaching and waved back. He bounded off the stage and came back and gave me a big hug. I didn't know how to get in touch with him so I hadn't told him we were coming. "Brother Chuck," he beamed. "Brother Chuck." The whole congregation turned to look back. And when they saw the gang of white boys walking down the aisle with Charles they gasped out loud.

Charles ordered chairs to be set up on one side of the stage for us and we got up there and sat down. We must have looked like a jury of one's peers. Brother Charles was effusive. "Brother Chuck. Brother Chuck you finally came to see me. I'm so happy. Everybody this is my friend, Brother Chuck. He's a good boy. He's come to see us with his friends. I'm so happy. Say hello to Chuck and his friends" He did a little shuffle with his feet and broke into song. A tinny trumpet, rhythm guitar and snare drum combo kicked in and the congregation chimed in singing: "Oh Lord, I'm working on a building, Yes Jesus. Thank you Jesus"

My friends and I looked at each other. Smitty and Kenny, always the hams, started waving at the people and they waved back and we laughed and they smiled, so things were good.

Charles wore black slacks and a pressed long sleeve white shirt open at the neck. He was sweating and had his handkerchief out. He told the congregation some of the conversations we had had. He told the people again what a good boy I was even though I persisted in believing that the world was round. Everybody laughed and he winked at me.

Then he turned to me and asked in a sympathetic tone, "Chuck, what brings you to our little church this Friday night. Does someone you know need our prayers?"

Man, that cut me to the quick. The place became very quiet. I stood up slowly and told everyone about my mother. I said that I had come to ask for everyone's prayers. I told them that I thought Charles was a holy man and that if anybody could help my mother he could. I said I didn't have anywhere else to turn. I looked around the church and felt that every person there was listening to me and taking my story to heart. When I finished I sat down.

Charles was standing alone in the center of the stage. He dropped down to one knee, put his head down and began to pray. I never saw a man pray with such feeling. He didn't have set words, he just talked to God out loud. He told God what a good boy I was. He told him what a great woman my mother was. He told Him how much us kids needed her. He said he knew God would help my family. He praised God for being all merciful, for being a God of love, for being a God who takes care of his children, a God who loves his children. He asked God to give my father strength. He asked God to give us children strength. He asked God to give my mother strength. Sweet Jesus, precious Lord. Yes, Jesus. Yes, Jesus. We love you Jesus. We love you Lord. Hmmmm, sweet Jesus. Thank you Lord.

The congregation was behind him yelling out "Amens," "Oh Lords," "Yes Lords," and "Sweet Lord have mercys."

Charles then went into a kind of state. He started shaking. Words began to burst out of his mouth that I never heard before. Fragments of songs flowed from his lips. You could see he was talking with God on another plane and I felt that this must be a plane where God listens to you and hears every word you're saying. The congregation started to sway and yell out more and shake their upraised hads at the ceiling. People started to jerk as they prayed and made whooping sounds.

Suddenly, after about five minutes, Charles stopped praying and stood up. He turned to me with a big smile on his face and I could see the sweat on his face under the stage lights. "Brother Chuck," he said, "your momma's gonna be just fine." He broke out into a shuffle-like dance and the little band kicked in big time and the people started singing and dancing and the place cut loose. Some people started running back and forth in the aisles, some were doing quick footed little dance steps, others were standing and swaying and clapping their hands. Others held their heads back with tears streaming down their faces. People were gone. As I looked over the congregation I saw a white guy standing in the seats. It was the Jewish guy. I'll be damned.

Smitty stood up and imitated people and Kenny followed his lead. They were both good dancers so they started dancing too. We all stood up because you just couldn't sit anymore. The place was supercharged and the noise was deafening.

In the midst of this pandemonium, Charles walked over to me and grabbed my head in his hands and gave me a hug. "Your momma's gonna be alright, Chuck. The peoples is doing their victory dance. She's gonna be alright. Praise the Lord. Thank you Jesus."

I felt happy. I couldn't have asked for anything more. I wanted with all my heart to believe what he said. I *did* believe it. I guess I did believe it. I couldn't wait to see my mother at home and our family back together. Charles's self-assuredness opened my heart. If I wasn't with my corner buddies, I probably would have cried like a little girl then and there.

We stayed on the stage until things quieted down and then we said our good-byes and made our exit. Charles walked us to the door and I gave him a big hug. I gave Leroy a big hug too and everyone else that was standing around. Charles invited us back any time and had his ushers accompany us to our cars so there wouldn't be any trouble.

We were juiced big time as we took off and blasted the radio at top volume. "My Boyfriend's Back," a Shirelle's tune that we all loved came on and we sang along at the top of our lungs. We kept the radio loud all the way back to Cicero. Everyone agreed the night had been a big rush. We had a couple of cigarettes on the Post Office steps and passed a jug of Chianti around and then I drove back to Westmont. The corner boys wished me well.

I couldn't wait to tell my father and the kids what had happened but when I got home all the lights were off and everyone was asleep. I knocked on my father's bedroom door. I didn't want to wake him but I couldn't wait until morning to share my news. After several knocks, the door opened slowly and he came out putting on his robe. His black hair was messed up from sleeping.

"Charley," he said softly with mild surprise, "What's the matter?"

"Nothing dad. Nothing's the matter. I just wanted to tell you something."

My dad stood there slump shouldered, his eyes deep caves in the dim light.

"Dad, listen, I went to my friend's church. These two black guys that I used to work with at Follett's. They're ministers and they have this church in Chicago. So I went there tonight and asked them to pray for mom and they did. The whole church prayed for her dad. And when they were finished, Charles, he's the main minister who's one of my friends, he said that mom was going to be alright. She's going to be alright dad. Isn't that great! Can you believe it? She's going to be alright!"

My dad just stood there looking at me, his face wracked with misery. Seeing him like that, my heart seized up and pitched itself off a cliff. What was I thinking?

"It was very nice of your friends to pray for mom, Charley," he said. He patted my shoulder, said goodnight and turned and closed the bedroom door behind him.

I went upstairs and moaned myself to sleep. The next week I lived in the lowest level of hell I had ever been in. In this place the demons gnawed in my gut twenty four hours a day, constantly ridiculing me for believing in God, believing in anything good.

To everyone's surprise, my father announced the following Saturday morning that my mother would be coming home for a visit in the afternoon. Seeing my mother was like seeing spring return to a dead planet. I stared at her all afternoon through a blur of hot tears. My father had to keep the little kids from climbing on her because she looked so weak. It was a thankless job. That night my mother refused to go back to the hospital. My father talked to her doctor over the phone. Nobody wanted to fight with her because any strain on her heart could kill her.

My mother refused to leave on Sunday as well. She refused to leave on Monday or Tuesday. And so it went. In another couple of weeks my aunt Kate brought the little kids back home and my mom began to take care of them again. My dad got upset with her as much as he could when he got home from work because she had done the laundry that day, or had vacuumed a rug, or was standing in the kitchen too long making supper.

My mom raised all her kids. She didn't have a wheel chair or live-in nurse, none of that. She died only after baby Dave had grown up and turned twenty-one. I was with her when she died in the hospital. She asked me if I believed in God and it was okay to die. I kissed her cheek and told her it was. About an hour later she was dead. The doctors said that her diseased heart had totally destroyed all her organs. There wasn't anything left to save. I knew that the last twenty-one years of her life was a miracle.

I never saw Brother Charles again after that eventful night. Time slipped by and the miracle of my mother's life became common place, just as the miracle of life becomes common place to each of us. Even so, Brother Charles still lives in my heart as the man who showed me a real miracle and saved my mother's life and the life of my family to boot.

Why didn't I become a member of Charles's church? I just couldn't do it. Even though I knew that Charles's connection to God was one hundred times more powerful than anything I had seen in the Catholic Church, the idea of going to the Southside of Chicago every

Friday night was too preposterous. God graciously left me off the hook by not riddling me with guilt for being weak and spineless. I thanked God by promising I would take my own religion more seriously. It was the first deal that I had ever cut with God. Not much to speak of. Wimpy. But a deal nonetheless.

I was going to Illinois Benedictine College at the time. It was a men's college. Some of our fellow students were studying to be priests. Everyone was really cool or at least fun to razz and make fun of. Every student had to take a bunch of theology classes. Some of the books we read were good but it was so intellectual. I easily got bored with religion and, the truth is, I blew my deal with God. I couldn't even keep a wimpy deal.

After seeing God shine in the face of Charles Little, those Catholic theology classes and going to mass on Sunday just couldn't cut it anymore. Charles was the first spiritual master that I ever met. There was no comparison between him and a priest, even the holiest priest I had ever met. And one more thing, white racists who think Blacks are inferior are full of it. The two great divisions between people that I had learned as a child were both based on irrational, self-serving nonsense.

Part Two

The Wave Of Love

The Guru

I finished my last year at college in 1967 and found myself working for the Department of Public Aid on the Westside of Chicago. The Westside is the new black ghetto, populated by the great migration of people coming up from the South that began as human labor was replaced by tractors on farms and plantations after World War II. People just kept coming. The Westside is more restless and violent than the Southside where the black population is more settled and middle-class. My Public Aid caseload consisted of about two hundred families receiving Aid for Dependent Children, all of them in a two-block area. Most cases were single women. If caseworkers saw any evidence of a man in a household, we were to report that and the welfare check would be stopped. The rationale of the government was that a man in the house should be able to take care of a family by getting a job. The reality was that there was one job for every two men on the Westside. With fifty percent unemployment, the expectation was ridiculous and punitive. It was a way for the government to keep the people suppressed and make it impossible for strong families to be built. More boys without male role models meant more street crime and more jail sentences. They fed the state's criminal justice system and created a lot of jobs for white people in rural areas.

My area is in a section of the Westside called Miles Square. It isthe poorest, most desperate square mile in the city.

It has been a hot year. Race riots have destroyed entire neighborhoods in Detroit, LA, and Newark. During the summer, younger, more militant leaders, including Stokely Carmichael and H. Rap Brown, are preaching armed confrontation as a means for Blacks to achieve justice. Huey Newton and Bobby Seale have founded the Black Panther Party for Self-Defense late in 1966. The White segregationists are looking to George Wallace, the former Alabama governor who had blocked school integration in his state, to run as an independent presidential candidate.

Voices of reason are beginning to wonder aloud if Martin Luther King, a recipient of the 1965 Nobel Peace Prize, had lost the initiative for social change through non-violent protest. Confrontation is now becoming the name of the game.

Martin Luther King speaks in Memphis on April 3, 1968. Joining striking black sanitation workers, King recalls the long civil rights struggle. He notes the countless sit-ins, the freedom rides, the marches in Selma and Birmingham, and confrontations with police. He speaks of the triumphant gathering at the Lincoln Memorial in Washington, D.C. where hundreds of thousands gathered to hear his exhilarating voice proclaim a dream in which one day soon, "the sons of former slaves and the sons of slave-owners will be able to sit down together at the table of brotherhood."

And on that day in Memphis, King spoke of no longer fearing death because God had led him to the mountaintop. "I may not get there with you," he said to the rapt audience, "but I know tonight that we, as a people will get to the Promised Land."

On April 4, one day later, King is murdered. For weeks afterward, riots, arson and looting erupted around the country. Newark, Trenton, Pittsburgh, and Baltimore suffer heavily. Fifteen-thousand troops are called into Washington, DC where arsonists light fires within blocks of the White House. In Chicago, police receive their orders from Mayor Richard Daley: "Shoot to Kill."

The long, dreadful summer had begun. It would take years to rebuild cities and to heal wounds.

Being a caseworker in the slummy Miles Square area on the west side of Chicago turned me into a revolutionary. I realized that the purpose of public assistance was not to help people get on their feet, it was to regulate their lives and to ensure that the great majority would never succeed. The economy did not need them and they would never get jobs. The blacks were used by the ruling elite as a threat to the white lower and middle class to work harder lest the blacks come and take their jobs, their daughters, and their neighborhoods. I had seen this white racist strategy work my whole life—"the niggers are coming!"

In Miles Square, I work a two square block area with over two hundred cases. Each case is more desperate than the next. On the day that Martin Luther King Jr. is shot, I was trying to get Lovey Shorty and her children a new apartment. She is living in an abandoned building where the roof had caved in and the winter snow and ice formed a glacier that ran down the bathroom wall and out into the hallway. Lovey and her kids live in a tiny kitchen crawling with cockroaches and uses the gas stove for heat.

There is not enough money for rent in the welfare allotment even for apartments in the poorest sections of the city. I learn that even getting a small allotment for kids clothing was difficult beyond description. Identifying with my clients' lives filled me with such anxiety, depression, and frustration that my doctor recommends that I start taking Valium. I can't explain to my wife or any of my middle-class friends about the horrors that I see. They couldn't understand.

The day that Martin Luther King was shot the people in Miles Square rioted. A large crowd gathered several blocks west of our building on Madison Avenue. They marched east down Madison Avenue smashing windows and burning stores. We could hear the din and see the black smoke rising in the sky from our office windows on the fifth floor. I watched as several squad cars arrived out front with their red and blue lights swirling. The police surrounded the building and began evacuation procedures floor by floor. By the time we got out, I could make out the mob coming down Madison less than two blocks away. One of the guys in my crew gave me a lift into the Loop where I took a subway train back home.

We were back at work the next day. People acted as if nothing had happened. Neither the caseworkers nor the clients wanted to open the subject. I was still taking Valium. My problem was that even though I knew the poor people weren't equal in knowledge and skills to the middle-class professionals that regulated their lives, they were still equal as human beings. As such, I took their suffering and their humiliation personally.

One day, after being on Valium for about a month, Bob Lavery, a fellow caseworker in my crew, told me about yoga. He said it might reduce my stress. I bought a book "Yoga for Americans" and started to do the book's exercises when I got home from work. It helped me. I was soon able to calm myself by my own will power. I got off Valium. After about nine months as a caseworker, I knew in my bones that the so-called welfare system was oppressive, repressive, suppressive, and deceptive in its intent. There wasn't much I could do as a caseworker to make peoples' lives better. My colleagues felt the same way. This was why the turn-over rate among caseworkers was so high and why even the best intentioned and hardest working caseworkers became hard-boiled and cynical over time. It is still this way today.

In Chicago, in the fall of 1968, the Democrats hold their National Convention in the Chicago Amphitheatre. Mayor Daley is determined to use an iron fist to handle any protestors. One evening there are about ten thousand demonstrators in Grant Park on Lake Michigan. A young boy lowers an American flag and the police break through the crowd and begin beating him. The crowd responds by throwing food, rocks, and whatever else they can find at the police. The chant of the crowd changes from the anti-war "Hell no we won't go" to the "Pigs are Whores." A lot of blood is spilled that day and the tear gas was so thick that Hubert Humphrey, the Democratic Presidential Candidate, inhales gas while taking a shower in his room at the Hilton Hotel across the street from Grant Park. As the police run around beating people, the news channels take footage of the carnage. These shots become the most famous images of the Chicago convention. During the mayhem the crowd continues to chant, "The Whole World is watching." And indeed, they are. For the first time the people of the world can see how the empire that bullied the world, now bullies its own people.

I was in Grant Park that night and was beaten with a baton and sprayed with tear gas. I had a gun put in my face. This all happened within a minute of coming out of the subway stop in Grant Park. I hadn't done a thing.

In the fall of 1969, I enroll in graduate school at Southern Illinois University (SIU).

I need a break from the harsh reality of Chicago's ghetto streets and I find it in sex, drugs, and rock 'n' roll. I am not alone. Carbondale, the home town of SIU, was becoming the Midwest epicenter of the emerging Hippie culture. I decided I wanted to be a Hippie. At the time, the social climate was still controlled by the fraternity and sorority houses that were "rushing" their recruits and having outrageous drinking parties, but on the fringes, Hippies began to appear. By winter break there were about one hundred of us. It was easy being a Hippy. You just got in a conversation with someone, it didn't matter where, smoked a joint with them, and became friends for life.

On Friday nights, a group of us usually got high, played Risk and laughed ourselves sick on the floor of Grape and Botch's room on Elm Street. Grape, a chunky blond kid with a cherubic face, would turn off the lights, put on the black light and switch on the stereo. Botch lit the pipe and passed it around the room. We got blasted listening to Jimi Hendrix, the Doors, the Jefferson Airplane, and Janis Joplin. Our common bond was that we knew what Jimi meant when he asked "Have you ever been experienced?" We knew that our parents were not "experienced" and would never be. We had crossed over a mystical bridge, a generational divide and we would never go back again.

The farm boys from central Illinois who made up the majority of the kids in the boarding house thought we were "real weirdos" and expressed obvious disgust. Over time we turned them on too, and soon the Risk game moved into the living room. Every Friday night became a big party with reefer and beer. Kids would pass through the living room to take turns at conquering the world. We dropped little colored tablets of LSD that came into town from California, Massachusetts, Mexico, India, and Morocco. We lived in a "far out" universe that was different from the one that our parents, teachers, and cops lived in. We wore weird clothes. We let our hair grow long. The Cultural Revolution had begun.

One day, I saw a poster saying that a yogi from India was going to give a meditation class at the high school gym on campus. I remembered my yoga postures from Chicago. If yoga postures could help me calm my body, who knows what meditation could do.

"Learn the science of self-realization," the poster said. It could be like dropping acid, I thought, but without taking chemicals. Timothy Leary, a Harvard scientist, and Ram Dass in "Be Here Now" had said as much. The thing that acid did was it stimulated the pineal gland. Otherwise this gland is only active in the higher states of meditation. "I'm going," I told myself.

The meditation class is packed with a couple of hundred college kids sitting on the gym floor. The yogi is dressed in bright orange. He tells us his organization is called Ananda Marga, "the path of bliss" and his name is Acharya Vimilananda Avadhuta. He says we can call him "Dada," which means "brother." That's a relief.

Dada teaches us a little dance that he calls kiirtan, with a side-to-side movement and our arms raised to heaven. He also teaches us a couple of chants and then he teaches us how to meditate. The lights are turned down and we sit in silence.

It is hard for me to concentrate. My butt aches. A girl to my side and a row up has nice legs and my eyes involuntarily kept opening to look at them. We meditate for a half-hour. It seems like two hours. Afterwards, I go with my friends to MacDonalds. Then we go back to Grape's, get high and talk about it. Everybody says it was far out. Nobody says how hard it was.

A couple of days later, Sabu, a speed freak from Lombard, Illinois, who has become a good friend, tells me that he knows where the yogi is staying and that we could go see him. He waves the address on a crumpled piece of paper. "Let's do it," I say.

The yogi is staying with a graduate student in Economics from India named Ravi Batra. Ravi definitely is not a hippy. He has short hair, wears straight clothes, and talks rapidly with a strong Indian accent. It is hard to follow what he says. Later Ravi is to become a famous economist with several books to his credit.

When we entered Ravi's apartment, we were invited to sit down. There were a lot of people sitting around on the couch and on the linoleum floor in the living room. Some guys gave us peace signs and nodded. The yogi was in another room "initiating" someone and these people were waiting to go in. No lights were on, and the people, if they did talk, were whispering. Sabu and I sat on the floor and checked the place out. The place was clearly sparse. No plants, no posters on the walls, no incense, no carpets, no stuff... too weird. Sabu and I looked at each other and decided to come back another time.

I go back a couple of days later by myself. The yogi is sitting on the couch this time, eating vegetables and rice. He has his turban off and his shiny black hair falls on his orange shoulders. He is watching the TV news and grinning. He acknowledges me with a nod and motions for me to sit down next to him. I immediately decide that I like this guy. His skin glows and he looked really happy. I hadn't seen a guy this happy since Brother Charles and Brother Leroy. He keeps eating and watching the TV. I begin to look at it too. It is the part of the news when they give the daily body count of the war in Vietnam. It is always the same. There are always two or three Americans killed but hundreds of Vietnamese communists killed. It pisses me off to listen to this bullshit. The yogi chuckles innocently. "Every day it is the same," he says. I didn't understand how he could laugh at such deliberate lies and cynicism, but it struck me that he saw the world through much different eyes than I did

We sat there awhile. Dada offers me some food, but I decline.

"Dada," I say "what do you find so amusing about the body counts?"

"Every day it is the same story," he says, trying to wipe some rice out of his beard, "don't you see?"

I looked back at the TV set. No I didn't see. What I noticed instead was a picture of an Indian man on top of the TV set with a slight smile on his face and a ballpoint pen in his shirt pocket.

"Who's that?" I asked.

"Huh? Oh that is the Lord," said Dada, his eyes becoming big with delight.

"The Lord?" I asked painfully.

"Shrii Shrii Anandamurti. Baba. He is our Father."

"Why do you call him the Lord?"

"He is the Lord of Lords," Dada laughs. I look at Ravi. He is grinning too.

That night Dada tells me stories of the "Lord." He says that "Baba," which means Father, came into this life fully conscious. Even as a baby, he knew everything and could do anything that he wanted.

"He has come," Dada says, "to make humanity one."

"How can you tell if a baby knows everything when a baby can't talk?" I ask.

"Like with everyone, you know him through his actions," Dada says bemused.

Dada told me two incidents to illustrate his point. When the baby was one month old, his family had a party for him. It was a traditional Hindu party, something like a baptism, where the child is welcomed into the community and offered to God as his own child.

During a certain part of the ceremony, the parents offer the child a spoonful of honey to signify that he should have a sweet life. But as Baba's parents held the baby to put the spoon in his mouth, the baby's chubby little hand took the spoon from his parents and fed the honey to himself.

The astonished family and neighbors stared in disbelief. Baba's mother began to sob deeply. She knew her son was destined for something she did not understand.

During the time that Prabhat (Baba's birth name) was a small boy, before he was old enough to attend school, a tiger would come to the edge of the jungle behind the boy's house. No one was aware of this happening except Prabhat. It was unheard of for tigers to be seen in the area and his parents did not worry about the child going in and out of the house by himself. They did not mind that he ran around the village at will.

Every day Prabhat would get on the tiger's back and ride him deep into the jungle. When Baba would return, and he was asked where he had been, he would tell his parents that he had gone to meditate. They thought it was cute and paid it no mind.

His parents eventually found out about the tiger. One day, when Baba was seven years old, he returned to his house riding as usual on the tiger's back. But this time his uncle, who had been working in the backyard, saw him.

As Baba dismounted from the tiger, his uncle ran into the house in a panic to get his rifle. He came out shooting at the tiger and the tiger retaliated by attacking him. They fought together and the tiger and the man killed each other.

"The graves of the tiger and Baba's uncle lie side by side in the village to this day," Ravi concludes the story. "Many people go to meditate at this site and when Baba returns to Jamalpur he always goes to the grave site and meditates there himself."

In the years following my meeting with Dada, I would hear many stories about Baba Anandamurti. Carbondale would become a base in the United States for Ananda Marga, Baba's yoga organization. As different monks and nuns passed through, they each had their own stories about the Master.

There was, for example, the story above the English woman who became deathly ill and swears that Baba was the doctor who operated on her in a London hospital and miraculously saved her life. Her Indian husband was a disciple of Baba's. He was in India doing business when he received word of his wife's illness and went to Baba to ask for His help. He was fearful that he could not make it back to London in time for his wife's emergency surgery. Baba had told him that he should not worry, his wife would be fine.

Another story was that of the angel-faced nun who told us how Baba had saved her from being raped by a gang of thieves one night on a lonely road in Mexico.

There was also the story about the monk whom Baba raised from the dead.

Over time, I would hear hundreds of personal stories told to me by disciples. They were miracle stories that changed people's lives forever. They were stories like the ones I am about to tell you now; for I too have had the experience of meeting Baba and have stories to tell.

Baba's Coming

In the spring of 1979 word came to us that Baba Anandamurti intended to come to the United States. Would he come to Carbondale? After all, by now we had created the strongest Ananda Marga community in the United States.

It is hard to tell how the ideas of Shrii Shrii Anandamurti transformed a group of pot smoking hippies into a committed band of social activists, but that is what happened. We had a strong core of thirty or so young men and women. By 1975, we owned our own meditation center. We had another large house where we ran a group home for troubled teenagers. We owned a school in another town. We taught preschool and kindergarten classes and literacy classes for the migrant workers who came up from Mexico every year to pick peaches and apples in the local orchards.

Our other projects included a mobile medical van that visited the migrant camps and small towns to give physical examinations to the poor. We had a food coop and an energy audit team that helped people winterize their homes. We also taught yoga classes in three state prisons in the area—Menard, Vandalia, and Vienna. In addition, we went to Marion Federal Penitentiary once a week. At the time, it was the highest maximum-security prison in the country. Three types of prisoners were kept at Marion. There were political prisoners like Leonard Peltier, major bank robbers and the like, and dangerous lunatics who were capable of anything. We met one madman who came to our yoga class who had ritually eaten the heart of another man.

Through his books, and through the monks and nuns whom he sent out, Baba Anandamurti had introduced us to a new Ideology that was a potent blend of spiritual science and social science. His motto was "Self-Realization and Service to Suffering Humanity."

These were two goals, that when integrated, offered the best life for the individual and the society. Baba called for the emergence of spiritual revolutionaries and this is who we wanted to be.

While we meditated and ran our social service projects, we also honed our ideas about social transformation. Baba's ideology included a spiritually-based political-economic theory called Progressive Utilization Theory (PROUT) that stood in sharp contrast to the materialism of capitalism and communism. He did not denigrate the material condition as many spiritualists do. He argued that to have the luxury to pursue God required that people first have their basic needs met. Baba defined these as food, shelter, clothing, health care, and education. These, he said, were our birth right at this stage of human evolution. Prout advocated the maximum utilization and rational distribution of all the Earth's resources and all human resources, be they spiritual, intellectual or physical, for the benefit of all.[1]

Baba stated that the highest achievement of human beings was God-realization. As such, he advocated that we organize our political and economic systems to allow us to achieve our highest potential. Baba turned the material worldview of capitalism and communism on its head. Instead of envisioning life as fundamentally a material construct, he argued that it is fundamentally a spiritual construct.

Matter, he stated, possesses no inherent dynamism of its own. It could do nothing unless activated by an outside force. Only consciousness is inherently dynamic, he argued. It is consciousness that gives birth to and activates matter, not vice versa.

We had many debates with the Marxists at the University and in the prisons about this theory. Many had become our friends and

---

1   For more information on PROUT go to http://www.proutinstitute.org/, or https://prout.info/.

Baba's spiritual ideology came under strict analysis by the Marxists. Being in a revolutionary state of mind and knowing the brutality of the capitalist system, I was not strongly inclined to the airy-fairy mindset that defined many of Baba's followers. In fact, I chose to call Baba, Mr. Sarkar, which was his birth name—Prabhat Rainjan Sarkar. In the process of ideological debate and creating service projects, we honed our vision of an improved social system. We sought to build a system that balanced the needs of the individual and the collective, the needs of humanity and other species.

At the time that news came that Mr. Sarkar was coming to the United States, I had been reading the works of Mao Tse Tung. I read his thoughts on dialectics, on politics, on economics, on military operations. The more I read, the more in awe I became of Mao. While many of the Marxist themselves rejected Mao because of his treatment of the intellectuals during the Cultural Revolution, I defended him. For me, it came down to one thing. Here was a man who underwent terrible suffering to build an organization that eventually was able to provide basic necessities—food, shelter, clothing, health care, and education—to over one billion people, one-fifth of humanity.

While I was later to learn that Mao was a murderous sociopath, at the time, I questioned if Mr. Sarkar, Baba, had the power and the presence of mind to provide a billion people with their basic needs. In my personal life, meditation took a back seat to the job of building an alternative political economy. While I was attracted to Prout theory, I was at this time more of a Maoist than a Proutist, more of a materialist than a spiritualist. I thought that maybe spirituality was too wishy-washy to get the hard work done. Maybe we wouldn't be able to draw enough proponents to Prout. It was, after all, a much tougher sell than simply pointing out the bad guys and going after them. Mr. Sarkar's coming might settle this core dilemma for me once and for all.

Jamaica

It p***ed me off when we received the news that the State Department would not let Mr. Sarkar into the United States. It did not surprise us though. He had proven to be an outspoken critic of international capitalism, but the real problem originated back in India where Baba had taken a hard stand against the corruption of the Congress Party headed by Indira Gandhi. Many people in the bureaucracy had now become Ananda Margiis and began to speak out against bribery and criminal activity in Indira's government. PROUT, as a political theory, was beginning to gain proponents.

Mr. Sarkar was also hated by Jyoti Basu, the Chief Minister of West Bengal, who was the leader of the Communist Party of India. Basu was worried that Prout might replace communism in the mind of the village people. The Russian secret service, acting in consort with Mr. Basu, also schemed to destroy Ananda Marga and Prout. Our enemies in West Bengal would stir up the local villagers with whiskey and money. They planted the idea in their simple, superstitious minds that Ananda Margis stole babies and would eat them in ritual sacrifices. Many monks and nuns were attacked by crazed men and hacked to pieces in public.

Indira Gandhi, the head of the Congress Party that ruled India, ultimately declared a "State of Emergency" in India to protect the country from "internal disturbance." The Emergency was in effect from June, 1975 until its withdrawal in March of 1977. The declaration bestowed upon the prime minister the authority to *rule by decree*, allowing elections to be suspended and civil liberties to be curbed. This action was basically an assault against Ananda Marga organizations, although Indira Gandhi also went after the Naxalites, who were Chinese communists. They were however, a small and marginalized group used as a cover for her true intention. Essentially, Mrs. Gandhi wanted to destroy Mr. Sarkar and his organization.

Earlier, in December 1971, secret agents of India's Central Bureau of Investigation threw Mr. Sarkar in jail on trumped up charges, accusing him of murdering six ex-disciples. By such means, the government was able to keep him in jail for seven years until each murder case was dismissed as a sham. It was not Indira Gandhi's intent, however, to convict him of murder. She wanted him dead.

On February 12, 1973, Mr. Sarkar was poisoned in his cell by the prison doctor in Bankipur jail in Patna. The poison was a lethal dose of barbiturates, administered in his food. It was enough to kill any man, but it didn't kill him. Not only did he survive the poisoning but in protest, Mr. Sarkar went on a fast. He refused all solid food from the jailers or his disciples until he was released from jail over five years later. In retrospect, I have never heard of anyone, sage, saint, or popular leader, who could have done such a thing. It was another one of those things about Mr. Sarkar that ranked with the miraculous.

When Indira Gandhi's State of Emergency was declared in 1975, Ananda Marga monks and nuns were also hunted down and imprisoned. Many were tortured. Some were butchered and killed.

It was only after Indira Gandhi fell from power, that her successor lifted the ban on Ananda Marga and released the nuns and monks from prisons. They returned to their schools, orphanages, clinics, and farms to find their buildings destroyed and their contents looted.

During this period of persecution, the Central Bureau of Investigation of India spread the word around the world that Ananda Marga was a dangerous terrorist cult. Newsweek carried a story naming Ananda Marga among the world's most dangerous terrorist groups. The State Department of the United States banned

Mr. Sarkar from entering the country. In 1978, the government of India's case against Mr. Sarkar fell apart when people he was supposed to have murdered walked into the courtroom to testify they were still alive.

Fortunately, the socialist government of Michael Manley allowed Baba to enter Jamaica and in 1979 Ananda Margiis in the US made plans to hold a retreat and meet Baba there.

We had no second thoughts about going to Jamaica. About twenty of us from Carbondale went and the hardcore Proutists were well represented.

Jamaica is a lovely country. It struck me to see that all the exotic house plants in Carbondale were growing outside in Jamaica, some as big as trees. The retreat site was a hotel in the hills outside of Kingston. We registered in the afternoon and sat around on the veranda, or by the pool drinking Cokes and waiting for the evening program at which we would have our first glimpse of Baba, the spiritual master.

Seeing Mr. Sarkar

My friends and I got to the hall early so we could sit up front on the floor, close to the dais on which Baba would sit. It was a good idea because the place filled up fast. Soon there were about four hundred people in the room quietly talking and laughing. Expectations ran high. Nobody here, outside of a handful of monks and nuns, had seen Baba before.

Suddenly two sharp cracks of a pole hitting the wooden floor filled the hall. Everyone became instantly silent. From the right side of the room we saw two men in khaki uniforms with gray berets carrying poles and marching slowly in step. Behind them walked a small man in white. He was only five feet three inches tall. His head was balding. He moved slowly. I watched him intently as he crossed the front of the room. There was definitely something about him. When his escort reached the dais, they assumed standing positions on either side of it. Baba sat down on the dais and folded his legs under him.

I will never forget his presence. He had a stillness to him that sucked in your attention. His eyes took in every detail of the room and the people in it. I was mesmerized and didn't know why. Later I realized that I was looking at a being who expressed no wasted movement. Not an unnecessary turn or hesitation, not a nervous tick, not a muscle, not a finger nor eye that moved on its own. This man was in perfect control of his body. Today, I have lived in New York City for twenty years and I have seen over a million people with my own eyes, but I have never seen a man like this. Neither before, nor since.

I was sitting a few rows back from Mr. Sarkar and a little to his right. His eyes began to scan the roomful of people who had gathered to meet him. Starting from the left of the room his eyes began a steady pan of the crowd. I watched his eyes come closer to me like the steady sweep of a flashlight beam. When they were about to contact my eyes, I couldn't look at him. His presence and bearing were too commanding. The thought came immediately that this man could do anything that Mao could do and more. We all knew we were in the presence of something extraordinary and he hadn't even opened his mouth to speak.

When Mr. Sarkar, Baba, did speak, the sound of his voice had an electric current to it. The sound itself created a buzz in you. But it was difficult to understand him. He talked about God but it was not in a personified way. He analyzed the nature of consciousness. What is consciousness? What is absolute consciousness? What is unit consciousness? How does consciousness become form?

What is relative reality? He raised and addressed these questions one at a time.

It was hard to follow him because I couldn't understand him. But I got an image of the universe being the body of God, while His mind was active in every particle of it and His soul witnessed everything from the nucleus of it all.

When Baba stopped talking, he told us to meditate. The hall became silent. We meditated for half an hour. Then Baba left, preceded by his escort. He walked slowly from the hall. My friends and I looked at each other. Holy shit! This was not a sweet kissy-face Guru. This was . . . .This was . . . .What was this?!

We went back to our rooms talking about how great it was going to be to hear Baba talk about Prout. Maybe we could even ask a question or two. Maybe he would even single us out as good examples of Proutists in America. I was twenty-seven years old and never met a hero in my life. What if Baba did know our innermost thoughts, what if he did know everything of the universe like people said? What if he was the embodiment of Divine Consciousness like the monks and nuns had told us? It was hard to go to sleep that night.

In the next couple of days, one side of my brain remained charged with the electric current of this possibility. But the other side of my brain was processing the days' activities and it did not like what it was seeing. I was frustrated. Baba, Mr. Sarkar, was meeting privately with people but he hadn't seen anyone from Carbondale. In the morning and afternoon, monks and nuns gave lectures on spiritual topics. In the evening Baba would give a lecture, but he never spoke about Prout. He only spoke about Paramapurusha—the Supreme Consciousness. His presentations were always like those of a lecturing professor. It never got any easier to understand him. He would talk and then leave.

We were getting toward the end of the retreat and though the buzz from people and the activities were enough to maintain a level of expectation, events did not prove favorable to the Proutists from Carbondale. Baba still had not seen any of us personally and we were feeling left out. Maybe our work did not please him. Maybe we were too insignificant for him to devote any attention to. Back in our hotel rooms, we stopped discussing Prout because there was nothing new to discuss.

We found out that people were chosen to meet with Baba by the monks and nuns who decided that they were doing good work in their communities. Baba would then tell them who he wanted to see. Dada Yatiishwarananda, who was the monk who headed the region of North America, assured us that he had submitted our names for personal meetings with Baba.

On the next to the last day in Jamaica, we heard that Mr. Sarkar had met with someone from Carbondale. Actually, he was a guy who used to live in Carbondale, but was now studying in Indiana. His name was Tim. He was not a Proutist, never did social service and wasn't "one" of us. He was sort of a sappy guy. Nice, too nice. Too sweet. But grudgingly we admitted that he was very devotional.

Carey Burke and Chris Perl, two Prout organizers who came with me from Carbondale, and I approached Tim at lunch and asked him about his meeting with Baba. He was starry-eyed in love. He told us in even more exaggerated and mellifluous tones than normal how Baba had taken him on his lap and told him how much he loved his little boy. Tim told us that he felt like he was in heaven. We tried to listen but we couldn't get the image out of our minds of this six foot four inch guy sitting on little Baba's lap who was only five foot three inches." It was too sappy and frankly depressing.

Tim did tell us something of interest however. The meetings with Baba were held in an apartment building a couple of miles down the road from the hotel. He said that a bunch of people were always hanging around in the apartment and that one guy who didn't have an appointment actually got in to see Baba. If nothing else, if we went there, we might get a chance to see him even if we couldn't get a meeting. It was something to do and we had nothing to lose.

We got directions to Mr. Sarkar's house and began walking down the hill. It was a hot day. The indoor plants were blooming everywhere. Dogs barked at us as we walked past houses set back from the road. We stopped to get a Coke in a little food store that had hardly any food on its shelves. It was the first Third World store that I had been in. Carey had been to Viet Nam so he grinned at me when he saw the look of surprise on my face.

A Swastika

The apartment where Mr. Sarkar was staying belonged to a disciple. When we got there, we found about twenty people sitting on the floor in the living room, others sat in the hallway by the bathroom door and down the hallway leading to Baba's room. His door was closed. Against one wall of the living room sat a small cluster of Indian women sewing green and blue sequins on squares of red cloth. They were putting the "Pratik," the symbol of Ananda Marga on the red squares. The Pratik consisted of an upward triangle intersected by a downward triangle to form a six-pointed star. In the middle of the star, sitting on the base of the upward pointing triangle was the semi-circle of a rising sun and within the sun a swastika. It was a powerful symbol, but to a Westerner disconcerting. It looked like the Jewish Star of David with a Nazi swastika in the middle of it.

We had told Dada Yatiishwarananda on more than one occasion how the elements of this symbol, especially the swastika held bad memories for Westerners, especially Jewish people. He looked blankly at us as if we were asking him to keep the sun from rising in the East and setting in the West each day. According to Dada, all the elements in the Pratik were ancient Tantric symbols. The upward pointing triangle, he said, represented the movement of the spiritual aspirant toward Divinity. The downward pointing triangle represented the love of God for the disciple. Where the two came into juxtaposition, enlightenment occurred. This was represented by the rising sun. The swastika, he said, meant success—success in enlightenment or God realization. It made a pretty picture, a powerful image that people would live and die for.

Dada said that "swastika" was a Sanskrit word. *Swa* meant soul and *stika* meant sticks. The vertical stick in the swastika indicated activity. The horizontal stick represented passivity. The feet on the end of the sticks indicated a perpetual rotating motion in which activity was continually transformed into passivity and passivity again into activity. This is the motion of the wheel of life, continually churning around its nucleus, represented by the single point in the middle of the wheel where the sticks cross each other. This single point represents the soul, the unifying principle and the witnessing entity of the drama of life.

Dada said the Nazis stole this rich symbol, perverted it through turning it on its axis counterclockwise and employed it in the service of evil. It was a good answer, probably all true, we thought, but it required a lot of education. As Proutists we felt uncomfortable leading a march with a flag having a swastika on it, or hanging a banner with the swastika on it in a meeting hall.

It was one of those key questions we wanted to discuss with Mr. Sarkar. We felt there needed to be some strategic decisions made in regard to this emotionally laden issue. Apparently though, it wasn't going to happen this afternoon. We hung around while Mr. Sarkar saw a couple more people and then a monk told everyone to leave.

I bought four of the little red squares from the women for a dollar each and we left.

We saw Baba again after dinner but it was the same as on previous nights. He was neither warm nor humorous. He presented a creation theory, in which an Operative Principle, acting on Unqualified Consciousness creates the universe by vibrating cosmic consciousness at different frequencies to form mental, then material waves in a step-by-step crudification process until the solid-state is formed. Trembling under awesome pressure due to this crudification process, the solid-state explodes in a big bang that creates the known universe. In this act, consciousness is atomized, giving rise to units of consciousness. Evolution is the process by which units of consciousness evolve through species to return to the Divine Nucleus." Baba defined yoga as the intuitive science by which human beings expand their unit consciousness to ultimately merge as one with Cosmic Consciousness. This state of unity is Self-Realization or God Realization.

It was, in actuality, an amazing vision and resolved many contradictions inherent in current worldviews, but by now, many of us Proutists had come to want more than theory. What happened to "God is Love"? Why did people say all those amazing things about Baba? Why did Tim paint a picture of him as so sweet and loving?

We left the hall that night intellectually stimulated, but spiritually vacant. Tomorrow would be the last day. The program was scheduled to be over at noon. There wasn't much time left for something miraculous to happen. Chris said he wished he had a reefer. It was a sacrilegious statement, considering the environment we were in, but we all felt the same way. It would be good to get back to Carbondale.

Baba's Darshan

When Baba came into the hall the last morning of the conference, he was even more business-like than usual. There were to be dancing demonstrations of kaoshiki by the women and tandava by the men. Kaoshiki was a yogic dance that kept your spine flexible and body healthy. Tandava was a warrior dance introduced by Lord Shiva and reintroduced by Baba. In the sculptures of Shiva as the Lord of the Dance, it is tandava that he is dancing in a ring of fire.

As we watched attentively, twenty-five women in maroon saris who had been sitting in the front row before Baba, rose up, gave their namaskar (spiritual greeting) to their guru and began to dance. They moved in unison while musicians kept the beat. They moved from left to right and back again in a continual motion. The ball of the left foot touched the floor behind the right heel and then the ball of the right foot touched the floor behind the left heel. As their feet moved back and forth, they extended their arms over their heads with their palms touching each other. From this position, they bent at the waist three times to the right, then three times to the left, then forward with their fingers touching the floor and then stretching backward as far as they could go. They then resumed the upright position, stamped their bare feet in unison and began the series of moves over again.

As the woman danced, the people chanted "Baba Nam Kevalam", ("the Expression of God is the only Reality") over and over to the beat. This lasted for two or three minutes. The women stopped dancing by stamping their feet quickly in unison. They gave Baba a namaskar and then quickly sat down. It was entrancing and beautiful to watch. Baba nodded approvingly and smiled.

Now it was the men's turn. They entered the hall from the left, bare-chested and bare-legged, carrying burning torches in their left hand and knives in their right. The air became electric.

The men formed three rows, eight men wide in front of Baba, who sat straight up now like a general surveying his troops. An absolute silence fell over the hall. A monk yelled out "Dancers ready."

The men rose on their toes in unison and extended their arms straight out to each side. Black smoke billowed from their torches and spread over the ceiling of the hall. The knives flashed in the fire's light.

"Ta Din Ta," the monk shouted out.

The men jumped straight up in unison and dropped to their haunches. They sprang quickly up again into a standing position with their arms still fully extended to their sides.

The monk called out "Baba Nam" and the dancers kicked their right leg across their bodies as high as they could and returned to the balls of their feet. "Kevalam" the monk called again and the dancers kicked the left leg across their bodies as high as they could.

"Baba Nam" Jump. Kick right.

"Kevalam" Jump Kick left.

"Baba Nam" Jump. Kick right.

"Kevalam" Jump Kick left.

Everyone in the hall chanted in unison and clapped their hands.

"Baba Nam"

"Kevalam"

"Baba Nam"

"Kevalam"

The pace became intense. The dancers kicked higher and faster. The chanting voices roared. The flames swayed and the black smoke streamed off the torches. The hall filled with smoke as the knives slashed the air.

"Danceeers Halt!" The monk cried out above the din and everything stopped dead. The dancers stood motionless. Their eyes straight ahead, their chests heaving.

"Ta Ta Din Ta" the monk called out one final time and the dancers took one more leap into the air, landed on their haunches and rose slowly in unison to a standing position. They lowered their arms, bowed to Baba and walked silently in a column out of the hall.

Baba nodded his approval. He raised his folded hands to his forehead in the traditional Indian gesture of acknowledging another's divinity and kept them there until the last man left the hall.

Normally Baba would give a talk before meditation but this time he closed his eyes. He sat straight like a Buddha with his palms crossed in his lap and didn't move.

Dada Yatishwarananda, the monk who organized the program seemed confused. We sat in silence for several minutes, our eyes glued to the little man in white. His face was expressionless. His body like a statue. A quiet peace slowly descended over the hall. It felt good.

Soon a lone voice began to chant the ancient Rig Vedic mantra "Samgachadwam" that began every Ananda Marga group meditation. Four hundred voices joined in, singing in Sanskrit:

Let us move together
Let us sing together
Let us share like sages of the past
That all people together may enjoy the universe
Unite our intention
Let our hearts be inseparable
Our mind is as one mind
As we, to truly know one another, become one.

After the chant was sung, the room fell silent. People began their meditation. It lasted for a half hour. It was no different than any other meditation. I repeated the mantra that was given to me by my Acharya (yogic teacher) during the first lesson of my spiritual practices. My mantra had two syllables. I would say the first as I inhaled and the second as I exhaled. The meaning of the mantra is "I am One with the One."

Typically, when people sit to meditate, they witness their own mind darting from thought to thought uncontrollably. They see it burrowing down wormholes of doubt, fear or anxiety. In contrast, the mantra is the biggest, simplest, all-encompassing thought the mind can think. The process is to bring the mind back to the mantra each time it has strayed from its focus. Through constantly disciplining the mind in this manner, concentration improves and the consciousness of the mind expands. As this occurs, the mind develops the force to progressively overcome larger internal contradictions. This allows the "I" to gain a deeper sense of identity, free from the prison of undulating waves of thoughts and feelings.

This is no easy task. In my own meditation, "I" was either thinking or not thinking and rarely had the presence of mind to know when I was doing either. I just thought or did not think. Sometimes I knew what I was doing, but most of the time I didn't. My mind just darted from thought to thought.

If you realize that you are God, you will be God, a monk once told me. But right now I was thinking that I didn't know what was going on. Baba had still avoided us. Basically, I was uptight. Having someone with the stature of an idealized Mao as a leader was no longer enough. I wanted more now. I wanted something I could believe in from the core of my being. I wanted love, I wanted peace, I wanted bliss. I wanted my Father, a Baba, who was unfathomable, who could take me all the way. I wanted to go beyond the melting walls and gritty joy of a hippy acid trip. I wanted more than what I could imagine in my wildest dreams. I wanted what Baba told me

I could have—limitlessness. This is what I wanted. Nothing less than the promise of limitlessness would satisfy me now. It seemed an impossible dream.

As I sat there in that silent hall, my knees throbbing, my ass hurting from several days of meditation on a hard, wooden floor, my heart collapsing like a dying star, the thought of my mantra entered my mind. What was my mantra saying . . . . My mantra . . . . What did it mean again?

"Nityam shudham, Nirabasam"

The chant to end meditation began. It startled me out of my internal morass. I joined the chorus to sing in Sanskrit the following words:

Eternal, Pure, Indescribable Entity
Formless, Without Blemish
Omniscient, Blissful Consciousness
To Guru-Brahma, Supreme Consciousness, I
Pay My Salutations.

It was now, at one of my lowest moments, when the most remarkable event in my life occurred.

Samadhi

A commotion began in the front of the hall. A girl who had been sitting in the front row closest to the platform on which Baba sat, yelled out his name and apparently had fallen over backward. People started moving toward her.

As I looked at Baba from the back of the room, I could see that something extraordinary was occurring. He was assuming a particular pose. His left hand remained in his lap, but he had raised his right hand with his palm facing outward. His thumb and index finger were joined in a closed loop and his other fingers were extended straight up. I could see his lips moving slowly as if reciting an incantation. I had seen pictures of Buddha in this pose. It now dawned on me that I was looking at the living Buddha. There was no mistaking it.

As I stared at him, I had the unmistakable sensation that something was opening up! An energy of some kind was being emitted from his raised hand. People started to wail, shout, and bounce. More people fell over. Some shouted out His name. Some laughed hysterically. Others blubbered and sobbed. My mind raced. My body froze. I could feel adrenaline racing into every cell of my body. What . . . Is. Happening!

Now I could discern a pattern. Whatever this force was that was coming from Baba, it was rolling out from him in a wave. I could see its impact now as it hit row after row of people. The hall filled with the noise of people in a spasm of something beyond comprehension.

"Baba, Baba, Baba" they yelled. The scene was becoming unglued.

"Sweet Jesus," I thought. The wave was now about fifteen rows from me. I could see a guy bounce up as if his spine was hit by a bolt of lightning and then fall over backward.

As I watched the wave rolling relentlessly toward me, I could feel my body hardening with adrenaline and my breath trail off into vapor. Every muscle was now taut as steel. Row after row it came, moving at about three miles an hour, no faster than a man walks. Six rows, five rows, four rows, three rows, two, one—the guy in front of me bounced up, screamed out "Baba!!!" at the top of his lungs and fell backwards, his head just inches from my folded legs . . . and then I felt it.

It did not come as a jolt, as I had expected, but seeped into me slowly like a gas, the sweetest, strangest sensation. My body began to tremble with tension. It instinctively wanted to resist this foreign invasion. But the more it resisted, the more the gas filled me up. It filled my guts; it filled my heart. It filled my arms and legs. My God! ... it was so sweet. It came and kept coming and would not stop. For some reason, my body still fought it, but it would not be contained, nor directed, nor influenced in any way. I was powerless against it.

It filled me up like a balloon and did not stop until I burst. Bang! I fell over backwards. But even now it did not stop. Wave after wave of this unimaginable thing surged through me. A river of sweetness flowed into every cell of my body eventually wiping out each remaining pocket of tension and resistance. In the end, I lay there saturated in bliss, every cell exuding ecstasy.

Although I was fully conscious, it did not occur to me that my mind had stopped reflecting, comparing, analyzing, complaining, or even enjoying. I was beyond the mind.

I don't know how long I laid there but when I opened my eyes, Chris, Carey, and Ray were staring down at me. The hall was almost emptied. They helped me to my feet and supported me back to our room.

I would remain in this heightened state of consciousness for the next two weeks. My life had been dramatically altered. I could not begin to know how. I didn't mind.

This was my second meeting with a Spiritual Master. Mr. Sarkar, I mean Baba, had given me my wish ... the taste of limitlessness.

Part Three

Inside Me, Outside Me

"Everyone received their brimful and felt contented. Everyone felt Him to be impartial. Incredibly, every disciple truly felt, "My Guru is my personal property." He gave each of us the feeling, "He loves me the most." Acharya Bhaskarananda Avt.

In 1980, our PROUT work in southern Illinois came to an abrupt end. Reaganomics cut $250,000 from our budget and left our projects decimated. We knew that the government could not be counted on to help people achieve a sustainable economy, but the day they pulled the carpet came too quickly. When it did, we were too few, too inexperienced, and had too few resources to create the economic infrastructure to support ourselves and help bring self-reliance to southern Illinois.

We began to lose organizers who could no longer find work in this rural area. Some people went to California; I chose New York City. I told the few of my companions who remained that I would spend a year or two in New York to research the global capitalist economy and improve our knowledge of how to build a local needs-based economy.

New York City, however, was much more difficult to cope with than I had imagined. I was intimidated by the buildings, the advertising, the incessant flow of strange people, the pace, the hardcore get over on the next guy mentality. I had few skills to survive here. My two thousand dollars that I had come with quickly evaporated. I took a minimum wage job selling refurbished oak furniture for a snarling hard-mouthed boss. I would sell a dresser for three hundred dollars that, in Carbondale, I could have bought for twenty-five dollars. I didn't understand the money here at all. I felt disoriented and humiliated.

After a year or so I got a job through my friend Shaam as a manager of a parking garage that was located in the basement of a twenty-story apartment building on Third Avenue and 25th Street. This provided me with a bigger salary and more security because I now became a member of the Teamsters union.

To make extra money I washed cars for ten dollars and waxed cars for fifty dollars and did other favors for my customers for tips. I quickly learned that in New York you didn't do favors for people to be nice. You did them because you expected to be compensated in some manner. This was the psychology and I learned to come up with "deals" and tell people up front what it would cost them. If somebody wanted to become a "monthly parker" in my garage, I would charge them one hundred dollars as a "key fee." This fee paid for me to submit their application to the owners. The company knew about my "fee," but it didn't seem to matter. The customers were glad to find a place to park and would never dream of making an issue of it. It was just "doing business" in NYC. Everybody expected it. Money was the connector here as opposed to neighborliness and a sense of community that was the connector in southern Illinois. It took me awhile to realize this so I got taken advantage of a few times during my first year in NYC. I would get angry at people for taking advantage of me until I learned to tell people that it would cost them if they wanted anything from me. After that it was okay. People respected me. I was one of them. They knew how to act around me. People would take my deal or leave it. Simple.

If a customer wanted me to park his car by the door for a quick exit early in the day, it was an extra five bucks. If a repairman wanted to park his van in the garage, it would cost him an extra twenty dollars a day for me to deal with the inconvenience. I was learning to be a New Yorker. In the process, however, my spirit began to shrink. My sense of humanity got warped as I began to see everyone as potential customers and every action of mine as a commodity to sell.

There were no Proutists in New York to help me keep my balance. There was an Ananda Marga center in Queens, but it was an hour by subway to get there and an hour to get back. My visits for weekly meditations were infrequent and then almost ceased completely.

While my Prout convictions remained strong, in reality, I am now slipping into a self-serving lifestyle. I am arguing politics in bars and at parties, but it is mostly for the sake of conversation because I'm not doing anything. I am interested in making money now and my contact with Carbondale is fading. The organization we built there has all but fallen apart. Ray has gone to Wisconsin, Chris and Steve are in St Paul, and Dean is in Colorado. Carey died from cancer contracted through exposure to Agent Orange in Vietnam. The women have scattered too, left for Chicago, California, and other parts. Chandra, Rita, and Maggie have stayed, but they all had kids now and were working for minimum wages, sliding back and forth on and off welfare.

At one point, Maggie came to New York to bring me back to Carbondale. I liked Maggie. She was a gorgeous red head and we had some of the steamiest times together that I'll ever remember. I did go back, but nothing was left and I couldn't stay alive there anymore. Things quickly went bust with Maggie and I found myself at the end of my rope.

My old friend Shaam, who had gotten me the garage job, came to visit me from New York. He was starting a new graphic arts business with a partner named Jan Suzanne and he wanted me to buy into the company. He said that Jan and he already had accounts in place that would pay my salary. I could even pay my share of the business out of income that I earned. While I hated the thought of returning to New York I had no choice.

Chandra and Anita helped me pack up the stuff in my trailer and we drove from Carbondale to New York in Anita's little red pickup truck with my stuff tied down in the back. When the women waved good bye to me after a couple of days of sightseeing, I got the blues real bad. It was now the late summer of 1983.

Commercial*ARTS*

We called the new graphics arts business Commercial*ARTS*. Jan was the art director. She was pretty and perky with a husky laugh and an easy way with people. She knew the graphics and advertising business. Shaam, my old friend, was big, gruff, outrageous, sexist, a rabid Zionist, and awkward with people. Initially, he'd bowl new clients over with a torrent of words that made you gasp. Blasts of intelligence, false bravado, bald lies, insanity, and vague threats mesmerized people and left them stunned. We tried to keep Shaam away from the clients, but it was hard because he needed to be the center of attention. His genius was that he knew how to grow a business and make sure that the lawyers and the accountants did exactly what we wanted them to do for a cheap price. He was the entrepreneur who had the vision, who risked the money, and who kept us on track. Later, as he became more sociable, he brought in some big clients from the real estate and insurance industries.

For my part, I kept the books, managing the freelance artists, and went out and got new business. We had a lot of small clients at first. After a while, I brought in a couple of big real estate clients and we put together high-end promotional books for them, complete with photographs, maps, and floor plans that we'd produce, so that they could sell their malls, housing developments, and skyscrapers. While most of our clients were courteous, including a few I could actually relax with, I was feeling more and more like a fish out of water. I'd sit in their oaken conference rooms, replete with oriental carpets, silk woven chairs, lush plants, and ten feet high windows that looked down on the vast chiseled world of Manhattan and we'd discuss how to sell other skyscrapers. This was not me. I felt like an imposter that would be discovered if I made a slip. I was definitely winging it. I didn't know the business; I didn't read the Wall Street

Journal; I didn't own any stocks or bonds; I didn't play golf. I didn't even know where to a buy good suit or a cashmere overcoat.

In my mind, I still longed for my little trailer back in southern Illinois with Maggie and her three kids. I could still see myself pushing our old clunker down the road to get it started, or looking for Seth's baby bottle behind the couch.

I was beginning to make some money though. I got my teeth fixed and joined a gym. I slowly began to feel comfortable in a suit and tie. In time, I got used to the endless stream of strange people I was meeting through the business. I didn't have any friends, but the endless chatter became a cheap substitute. Every once in a while, I'd even meet an unusual character like the sex goddess of X-rated movies or the he-man that ran the weight room down the block. Sometimes I'd see a movie star walking down the street.

A couple of years went by and I sank further into my New York lifestyle. I wasn't happy, but there didn't seem to be a way out. As this happened, I became less interested in Prout. I still meditated, but only occasionally.

My family life was also in transition now. I had begun to live with Ellen, after getting divorced from my first wife, Ruth, three years earlier. Ruth had moved to Chicago and our daughter, Flora, who was now eleven years old, was spending alternating years between us. This year Flora was with Ellen and me. I no longer had any friends around me, no sense of community, no greater purpose in my life than making sales tools for large real estate corporations in New York City.

Something was happening to me that I didn't like. My values were slipping away, and with them, my sense of self-worth. I wasn't even able to enjoy the time I had with Ellen and Flora. Then, out of the blue, one Sunday I received a phone call from an Ananda Marga monk inviting me to attend a group meditation that evening in Queens. It came at a time when my heart was a spiritual desert and it struck a chord. That evening I chanted bhajans, did kiirtan, and meditated again. Tears came to my eyes as I sat in silence and felt the full weight of my loneliness and alienation.

After meditation, we had dinner. We sat on the floor in a circle with pots, dishes, and glasses spread out on a tablecloth on the meditation room floor. I happened to be sitting next to a young monk, Dada Suprakashananda (su pra kash a nan da). As we ate, he told me that the guru, Baba, was holding personal one-on-one meetings again, and he was especially calling disciples from the West to visit him. "If you go now, you will be sure to have a meeting with Baba," he said, his eyes big like saucers to make his point.

Dada's words repeated themselves in my mind the next few days at work. I couldn't shake the idea of going to India. It had been almost ten years since Jamaica. But as I looked at my business partners, I knew it would be futile to ask them for permission to go.

In fact, we were in the midst of the biggest ad campaign we ever managed. We were working for Intelsat, a department of the United Nations that coordinated satellite communication between member nations. The chairman of Intelsat had decided to go toe-to-toe with AT&T and other multinational corporations to define the future of global communications. The race was on to find a single communications vehicle—an inter-systems digital network (ISDN) that could carry video, sound, and computer messages simultaneously around the world. AT&T and the private corporations were putting megabucks into fiber optic cables as the hardware on which to build the new system. Intelsat, for its part, wanted investors to put their money into satellite communications. Their argument was that satellites were a cheaper vehicle than fiber optics and more importantly, satellite technology could be made available to everyone, not just the rich nations.

The people from Intelsat were inspired by a vision of TV sets in tiny jungle villages linked by satellites that could offer education courses on any subject and help the vast majority of humanity to improve their ability to meet their basic needs of food, shelter, clothing, health care, and education. The corporations, on the other hand, wanted proprietary fiber optic cables because this would allow them to control international communications and make a profit.

For my partners and I, this was the kind of big project that could catapult us to stardom if we were successful in such a high-profile project. Our assignment was to create advertisements for newspapers and magazines that would be placed in the New York Times, Newsweek, Time, Washington Post, etc.

We had developed a concept that the people at Intelsat liked. We coined the term "ISDNvironment" and created an image of this new realm as being a lush garden viewed from grass level. In the grass, slinked ugly black snakes representing the fiber optic cables. In the sky, satellites floated like bees circling huge white flowers that looked like satellite dishes, their faces open to the sun. It was eye catching and clever.

On the Tuesday that followed my Sunday meditation dinner in Queens, we submitted the ad drawings and copy to Intelsat. Given the timeline, we knew that it would be a couple of weeks before they would get back to us with their comments. I knew that if I left for India during the next few days, and spent a week there, I would be back in time for the next round of work.

On Wednesday afternoon I got up the nerve to tell my partners that I wanted to go to India. As expected, they lost their minds. Shaam, who was hot tempered, threatened to call the partnership off if I left. I told them they had no choice in the matter. I had to go to India and get to the bottom of things. I had to know if God could really exist in a human body. I wanted to know if the distant memory of Jamaica was real or only a dream. By now, the "wave of love" had flattened into a distant memory. It did not make much sense in my new lifestyle. I wanted it to be real again. I could no longer count on its memory to fill me up and drive away the loneliness I felt.

The next afternoon, I took off early from work to get my shots of tetanus, yellow fever, and typhoid. On Friday morning I got my visa from the Indian embassy uptown and ordered my plane tickets. I told everyone that I'd be back in a week, not to worry. My partners were pissed and sullen. Ellen and Flora were confused and fearful. I couldn't blame anyone for their feelings and I felt bad for them, but I couldn't resist. Rarely does life provide an opportunity to resolve one's deepest psychological divide in one neat little package. I needed to know if God was real, or if Jamaica was a fluke. I needed to know what ultimately controls reality—matter or spirit. Which is more real? To which should I pay more attention? To which should I surrender my life? I needed to know the answer to these questions. If I didn't, I felt that I would remain alienated and unable to commit to anything in my life.

Baba's Supreme Command, which all disciples had to say at every group meditation, ran through my mind:

> *Those who perform sadhana (meditation) twice a day regularly, the thought of Parama Purusha (Supreme Consciousness) will certainly arise in the mind at the time of death. Their liberation is a sure guarantee. Therefore, every Ananda Margi will have to perform sadhana twice a day regularly. Verily is this the command of the Lord. Without Yama and Niyama (moral observances and abstinences) sadhana is an impossibility; hence the Lord's command is also to follow Yama and Niyama. Disobedience to this command is nothing but to throw oneself into the tortures of animal life for crores of years (reincarnations). That no one should undergo torments such as these, that everyone might be enabled to enjoy the eternal blessedness under the loving shelter of the*

Lord, it is the bounden duty of every Ananda Margi to endeavor to bring all to the path of bliss. Verily is this a part and parcel of sadhana, to lead others along the path of righteousness. Shrii Anandamurti

I was going to see the man who made up these words—tomorrow night. I'd be back in a week and jump on the Intelsat project again. I'd have some souvenirs for Ellen and Flora and some good stories to tell. I was getting psyched up.

In Kennedy Airport, while waiting for the flight to India to depart, I was surprised to see Dada Suprakashananda and another Dada whose name I forgot, but it started with the letter "R." They were also going for the trip. It made me realize how out of contact with the organization I had become, that I had not even called to let anyone know that I was going, or to find out if anyone else was going. In any case, the Dadas seemed pleased to see me and I was delighted to see them, considering I had no idea what I was going to do once the plane landed in Calcutta. The Dadas were laughing and in good spirits, happy to be going to see their Guru. Their happiness was infectious. They told me "Baba stories" until we boarded for take-off.

It was a Friday night flight. I had whirled around the last couple of days getting everything together and now as I sat in my seat, and the lights dimmed for takeoff, a great sigh escaped my lungs and immediately a strong feeling of disorientation. I felt like a baseball pitcher winding up for the pitch, his leg raised for the throw and then not remembering what he was supposed to do. What the hell was going on! I had left my partners smoldering, my wife and daughter worried beyond belief, myself dazed and feeling feverish from the frantic running around. I tried to meditate to calm my mind but couldn't. The last thing I remember before I fell asleep was my own mind saying "Dear God, help me."

INSIDE ME, OUTSIDE ME 69

It takes seventeen hours to travel from New York to India. When you add the clock adjustments for flying back across eight time zones, you end up getting to India the next afternoon, but it feels like it's taken forever. You've lost track of time. Your lower back is killing you; you've got a growth on your face; and you badly need a shower and sleep.

We had a couple of hour layover in Bahrain. Looking at sand as far as the eye could see felt strange and foreign. The airport was pleasant enough though, and I got together with the Dadas for cheese sandwiches in the airport cafeteria. This was our first chance to speak since takeoff, other than an occasional exchange of pleasantries when we stretched our legs and walked by each other's seats. It was at this point that Dada S. warned me that we might run into trouble in Delhi. He told me that even though Ananda Marga was no longer considered an enemy of the state, the Central Bureau of Investigation still tried to make life difficult for Margiis from foreign countries, by holding them for questioning during the customs check-in. Dada wanted to know if I had anything on my person or in my luggage that might identify me as a Margi. The only thing I could think of was a book of Baba's on Shiva that I had been reading on the plane. I was using it to put my mind into a spiritual framework again. Dada told me to leave it on the plane when we entered Delhi. I was to tell the customs officials that I was a businessman on the way to Calcutta for business reasons. He gave me the name of a hotel where I was to say that I would be staying. He also gave me the name of a company in Calcutta and a contact name there. "Well, here we go," I thought. I was wondering why the monks were wearing blue jeans instead of their normal bright orange garbs and turbans. Now I knew why. They both looked at me with wry smiles, these two, young blond Europeans. "Okay, I can deal with this," I thought. Those bastards better not kick me out of India as soon as I get there and waste my $1,500 ticket.

We got through customs in New Delhi without incident other than some nervousness standing in line with our baggage. The customs official I saw was doing a computer check on everyone. As he waited for the information to come up for me he asked my business in Calcutta. I gave him the information Dada had given me. There was nothing in the computer that connected me to Ananda Marga or any other red flag so I was waved through.

The Dadas also made it through without incident. The airport was big and busy and filled with fast food shops. Through a glass wall that separated the passengers from the outside world I got my first glimpse at India—a great press of humanity. Families looking for arriving kin, taxi drivers looking for riders, beggars looking for handouts. Soldiers with rifles stood guard. This is definitely not New York, I thought.

We had about an hour layover before our flight to Calcutta so we dropped our gear by some seats and congratulated ourselves for getting through customs without incident. I was feeling restless and decided to walk around. I found a currency exchange and traded a few travelers' checks for rupees. Unfortunately, I would discover later, that the large fifty and one hundred rupee notes I received would be virtually useless on the street where normal business was conducted in one, five, and ten rupee notes.

I also stopped and got a cup of tea from one of the fast food vendors. No one had coffee. The tea was very hot and bitter.

On the flight to Calcutta, the flight attendants made their announcements in Hindi and served us the usual Coke and peanuts. The Dadas and I were the only white faces on the plane. There were no bad vibes though, no stares, everything seemed normal. It was a sunny afternoon, we were all a little giddy from the trip, and our expectations were rising. It began to dawn heavily on me that I was in totally uncharted territory. New York seemed a distant dream. I tried to recall Ellen and Flora's faces but it was difficult. I slumped back in my chair and listened to the engines drone. I was going to see Mr. Sarkar. I was going to see the miracle man personally. What should I say to him? What should I ask him? Was he really God? If he was God how would I know it? Would he do a miracle again for me? Would he be glad to see me?

My stomach twisted into a knot. My heart began to churn. I realized I had a lot riding on this. I needed some magic in my life. I needed some love in my heart. I needed some conviction in my soul.

Tiljala

Calcutta was everything I imagined it to be and worse. From the moment I landed, I knew my world had turned upside down. The plane stopped on the runway. We exited and stood on the steaming tarmac and waited for a bus to pick us up. The air was hot and heavy and it stuffed your nostrils with an unforgettably sweet, sickening smell. It never went away all the time I was in Calcutta. It was a mixture of Sterno and cow dung, the two sources of fuel used for cooking meals in most households. Add to it a large cloud of vehicle exhaust and you get an idea of how Calcutta smells.

When we got to the terminal, we waited in a large cinder block room for our luggage to be brought from the plane. The room was crowded with people milling around looking at piles of baggage and cardboard boxes of all sizes that were all tightly duct-taped with names written in huge letters. The Dadas were attentively waiting by the big doors for our bags to be delivered. I decided that I had better pay attention too. All I would need would be to have my bags ripped off. When the truck came in the Dadas were all over it. We got all of our bags, which was a great relief and headed out of the airport.

Outside a mob immediately surrounded us. Many were beggars. Many were cab or rickshaw drivers. The long distance from the airport to Tiljala, where the Ananda Marga headquarters was located, ruled out every one but the cab drivers. The cabs did not have meters in them, neither were there published rates. This made every ride a fierce negotiation. Things could get ugly in a crowd of drivers. Dada S. made a quick negotiation, knowing from experience, a fair rate. We piled our gear in the trunk, while drivers continued to surround us yelling numbers in a language I didn't understand.

Calcutta is the largest city in West Bengal. The people are predominately Bengalis. They have a rich cultural and spiritual history, but colonialism badly beat them down. Today most of the people are small, thin, and gaunt from malnutrition and poisonous air. Their clothes are threadbare, faded, dirty, and wrinkled. People are everywhere. There are a few sad trees, but little else. In public areas anything green has long ago been stamped into powdered gray dirt and filth. A merciless sun eliminates most color.

The poverty of Calcutta is beyond startling. No movie could capture the feeling of this city. The worst scene you could produce on film would still look too pretty.

The roads in Calcutta were chock full of people, giant trucks with painted flowers, cars that all looked alike, goats, bicycles, rickshaws, motorbikes, cows, ox carts, an occasional elephant, you name it, all weaving in and out of each other. There were few road signs, no signs that identified streets. Few stop signs. It was a sea of chaos, oddly exhilarating, noisy, and rude. Everyone jutted in and out of traffic, missing each other by fractions of an inch, amid a deafening sound like a million lawn mowers revving in your ear.

All the buildings in Calcutta were badly stained from the air pollutants. Even the downtown area, looked stained and shabby.

This was clearly no place to vacation. Again, I thanked my lucky stars that I was with the Dadas who knew their way around. I envisioned myself traveling alone, being driven into a back street somewhere beaten and ripped off. I realized how unprepared I was for this trip. My New York cowboy Madison Avenue mentality got suddenly sucked out of me. I was in a serious situation here, Guru or no Guru.

The driver yelled something back to us that I did not understand. Dada R yelled back "Metropolitan By-Pass."

The Ananda Marga compound was located off the MBP on the eastern side of the city, in a slum called Tiljala. As the heat and noise poured into the backseat window, I watched the traffic and the emaciated cows sniffing in the piles of garbage that appeared along the road without rhyme or reason.

"We're close now," Dada turned to me grinning. "That's the sisters' compound over there." He pointed to a multi-storied mint green building out the left window. It was mostly hidden by a high concrete wall. In front of the wall was a large pool of water. It looked like many other pools I had seen on our cab ride that were left over from the rainy season. Three women knelt by the water's edge washing clothes while their kids splashed waist deep in the water.

In a minute we turned off the MBP onto a side street filled with people and little wooden stands. We stopped in front of a high concrete wall with a solid steel double door. The cab driver blew the horn and someone on the other side of the wall peered through a slot at us. Dada S. told him to open the gate. In a moment, both doors were pushed open by four men and we entered the compound.

We got our luggage out of the trunk and looked around us. The Dadas were grinning broadly. "Heaven," Dada R. said. I looked around at the shamble of buildings and scruffy, unkempt grounds. My heart sank. What kind of organization is this, I thought.

Underneath it all, I was thinking what kind of a Guru would live in this kind of environment. I thought of the cherubic faced Gurus who had come from India to live in the United States. Baba Anandamurti had these guys covered. No disrespect intended, why did he stay in this hell hole? I guess I knew the answer, but I wasn't ready for the implications of all this.

I was shown to a room by an Indian Dada. He proudly told me that there was a separate room for people who came from North America. For organizing purposes, Baba had divided the world into nine sectors. Each sector was provided its own room in the main building of the compound.

The room for New York sector was a large room, perhaps thirty foot by fifty foot with smooth painted walls and a polished stone floor. There were also many windows in the room, but the windows had no glass. They opened to the elements with only a decorated metal grating to keep out thieves or protect someone from falling out. The room was completely void of furnishings. A rumpled-up sleeping bag was thrown in the far corner. I rolled my sleeping bag out in another corner and got out some clean clothes to take a shower. The washroom consisted of a toilet without a seat, a small plastic bucket and a spigot that stuck out of the wall about knee high. A bare light bulb hung from the ceiling. The unfinished concrete floor was wet and dirty. This place was a pit that rocked my middle class sensibilities. Let's see. Where do I put my daub kit? Where do I hang my clean clothes? Where do I put my towel? There were no hooks or shelves.

Christ sake! I went back to my sleeping bag. Threw my clean clothes on it. Stripped, threw my dirty clothes on it. Grabbed my towel and a bar of soap and went back into the shower. I stuffed my towel into the metal grate covering the window so it wouldn't fall on the wet floor, picked up the plastic bucket, filled it with the cold water and threw it over my head.

The *shower* made me feel better. I meditated and laid down on my bag and began to read a book of Mr. Sarkar's that a Dada had given me. He had shown me to my room and told me that Baba was not staying at Tiljala but at his house in Lake Gardens. I was to relax today and tomorrow morning I could go with others into Calcutta.

My mind began to settle down and my mood improved. Reading a book of Mr. Sarkar's talks had a calming effect on me. The subject was how human beings as a species are transiting out of animality and moving into divinity in the evolutionary process.

As I lay on my bag reading, a young monk who I had never met before entered the room. He immediately sat down with me and began taking books out of his bag. As he took out each book, he put it in front of my face and told me what it cost. There was a small orange book with a red ribbon for a book market that attracted my eye. The title was "Light Comes." It was a collection of quotes from Mr. Sarkar, organized by category. I bought two books, one for myself and one for a gift. I offered Dada a fifty-rupee note, but he refused, saying he didn't have change. He said he'd rather have dollars any way. I gave him seven bucks. I wanted him to go away now, but he wouldn't. He kept sticking more books in my face until I got angry. When he realized he had pushed me too far, he backed off. Maybe before my visit ended, I would like to buy more books from him, he said. I glared at him and he left.

I dug in one of my bags and pulled out a large baggie filled with nut and raisins. I didn't know what time they ate dinner around here, but I was getting hungry. A minute or two later I was lying down and that was that. I was out for the day. It was the end of my first day in India—not exotic, not sublime. It was nerve-wracking, boring, and strange. It was only the beginning.

Lake Gardens

I awoke in pitch-blackness to the sound of distant drums. I could also hear faint voices. I listened intently and realized they were singing. They must be doing kiirtan, I thought.

I stumbled around in the dark to find my shoes, water bottle, and daub kit and went to the wash room to splash some water on my face and brush my teeth.

I was in a hurry because I realized that somewhere in the compound they were beginning group meditation.

When I entered the hallway outside my room, there were dim light bulbs that allowed me to see. I could now hear the singing coming from below me in the building.

I found about fifty people dancing in a large enclosed area under the building that could have accommodated hundreds of people. I can't say that it was a room, it felt more like a cave. The floor was dirt but covered with large plastic tarps. The back and side walls were open and the front wall and ceiling were solid unfinished concrete. The ceiling was only about six-foot high and this made me hunch over whenever I moved. The only light came from about fifty candles that burned on a wide, low table that contained a large picture of Baba Anandamurti. Both men and women were present, including monks and nuns and family people. The drummers were scattered among the dancers, holding their drums and dancing themselves. The shadows of the dancers leapt wildly on the walls and ceilings. As they danced, people sang the universal mantra "Baba Nam Kevalam"—love is all there is. Many people huddled in blankets to protect themselves from the early morning chill. The sun had not risen yet when the music stopped and we sat down to meditate. I fought to focus on my mantra against the cold air, the bumpy tarp, and my lack of discipline. At least I had gone to sleep early and was not tired.

When meditation ended, the darkness had broken. Outside the monks had brought a large pot of runny yogurt and piles of bananas. We lined up with aluminum plates and when we received our portions, we looked to sit wherever we could.

I looked around for Dadas S and R, but did not see them. I did meet a friendly man from Australia who said he was also going to Lake Gardens to see Baba and since he knew how to get there, I could travel with him.

It took a sequence of several forms of transportation to get to Lake Gardens. We began on foot. We walked the narrow street outside the compound gates to the Metropolitan By-Pass road and crossed it heading into a strange, almost stone-age collection of huts and shacks. In front of each hut that lined the narrow curving street was a small pile of items for sale. The first hut had a small pile of potatoes in front of it. As we walked by, I tried to look inside. I could see two people in the darkness. The only light that entered it was from the front entrance that was partially covered by an odd frame made with banana leaves that I guessed was the door, but was thrown up on the slant of the low curving roof. I couldn't tell what else I was looking at inside. It seemed like I saw a two by four frame of some kind, although I don't know what purpose it served. I could also see that the floor was dirt that had been blackened by the oil of food and human activity. This was the grossest, most abject poverty I had ever seen in my life.

The next hovel we passed looked similar to the first, but it had a small pile of bananas in front of its door. The next had a pack of AA batteries and an old TV set. I couldn't imagine it working, or if it did what you would possibly watch on it. I pointed it out to my companion who had the spiritual name "Purusottama" and he didn't think that anyone had access to electricity in the area.

After about a quarter mile of such huts, interrupted occasionally by an actual stand with goods, we reached the place where the rickshaw drivers gathered. We negotiated with a young man in a ragged tee shirt and dhoti for a ride to Hargath Bridge. From there we could get a bus that would take us the major part of the journey. We piled in the battered seat of the open rickshaw. As we moved along, I couldn't keep my eyes off the driver's legs. His calves were shapeless thin rods that worked like pistons pulling our weight over the dusty, pock marked road. Each bump shook the rickshaw. The frame would rattle and the thin tires would skid in the dust. This young man was working. I don't think I could have done it. He took us about a mile and a half. Where did he get his energy? Were the few rupees he got from us enough to get him through the day? How many more trips would he have to make? I noticed that he never smiled. Neither did he speak again after we had settled on the money.

When we reached the bridge, a bus was pulling up to the stop. We entered at the rear and Purusottama paid the conductor. He had paid the rickshaw driver too because my rupee notes were too large to be changed. The bus was old and battered, dirty, and crowded. The air was dusty and hot. Nothing looked good. Poverty and filth were everywhere. Nobody was taking a daily shower that's for sure. Men would wear their shirts for weeks, maybe months without washing. I guess there weren't any wash basins in those hovels, and then again who had money for soap.

When it was time to get off the bus about fifteen guys rushed at me. What the hell!? They only wanted my seat.

The last leg of the journey was a motorized rickshaw that dropped us off after a couple of miles in front of Baba's house.

So, this was it. Three days and thousands of miles later, I had finally made it. I now stood before the house of miracles. This was the place, according to legend, where Baba did many of his demonstrations to show the nature of consciousness. This was where he purportedly put a man to death and brought him back to life, and where he pointed two monks toward each other and withdrew their karma so that they cemented together in love. This could be the center of the universe. If it was, it didn't feel particularly supernatural this morning.

There was a wrought iron fence that separated the house and small courtyard from the narrow street that was more like an alley. In the courtyard there was space for Mr. Sarkar's old tan Mercedes that he had been gifted and a small paved area where people could stand outside the house. The house itself was a nondescript two-story rectangular building. To the right of the paved area, if you were facing the house, was a narrow band of thick vegetation containing trees and plants from around the world. Many were labeled. It was Baba's request that when his monks and nuns came to India for their reporting sessions, they bring him a plant from the area of the world in which they were stationed. It was one of the minor miracles around the place that Baba knew the identity of every plant that he received, including its utility and medicinal value. He also knew how to adjust the environment for each plant so that it would grow in Calcutta. Scattered around on the floor of Baba's little jungle, which also continued in the gangway and opened up again in a small backyard, were large glistening white rocks which I later learned were disks from the spines of dinosaurs.

Two doors entered the house. One was Baba's private entrance. The other, which had a large pile of shoes around it, opened into a garage-sized room with a stone polished floor. It was empty of furniture except for a small platform at the far end that was decorated with colored cloth. Behind it, on the wall, was a large "Pratik" in orange and white, the symbol of Ananda Marga.

I walked up to the platform, which was called a dais, and tried to feel its vibration. I didn't feel anything. It reminded me of sitting in church as a child staring up at the crucifix, wanting to feel God, but feeling nothing. Why does God keep himself [or herself] so invisible? We are supposed to give up everything for God and yet where is God when you need him?

It did not take much to make me feel alienated and cynical. As a spiritual seeker, this was not a good state to be in. I looked around the room. There were about twenty or so people standing or sitting in small groups talking at normal levels, occasionally laughing. A couple of people sat with their backs against the wall in meditation. Other than that, there was no other discernable show of piety. Every now and then a monk would come out of or go into a door beside the dais. Once when I peeked through the door, I saw a small, empty room with some built in solid wood cabinets. Someone told me the room was a kitchen.

I decided to meditate and get my center, but it was hard. I wasn't myself. I felt a little flush and I couldn't concentrate. The floor was hard too and I didn't bring a blanket or something soft to sit on.

After struggling to meditate for a half-hour I began to think how badly I had let my discipline slide. Meditating a half-hour twice a day was the minimum requirement of Ananda Marga. Now all I could think about was how my butt ached, how my knees ached, and how I couldn't get deeper in meditation than surface thoughts of discomfort and disorientation. How did I expect to have "Baba" make everything all right when my spiritual effort had been so pathetic over the last years? I was really feeling frustrated now and got up suddenly without doing the closing prayer. I tried to find a familiar face in the room and then walked outside in the courtyard but didn't recognize anybody there either. I thought that if I had been more active in the organization, I might know somebody.

Not everyone in the compound was Indian. There were several Europeans and Australians. They seemed engaged in their own discussions though. At the gate was a man who served as the gatekeeper. I asked him to let me out of the compound and to point me in the direction where I might buy some food or get a drink. He told me that if I walked to the left, in about five minutes I would find an outdoor market. I walked down the alley-like street looking at the houses. The neighborhood felt safe. The houses were middle class in appearance, but I knew that if you went inside you wouldn't find refrigerators, stoves, television sets, washers and dryers, that sort of thing. On each side of the alley ran a six-inch wide channel of waste water. That was new to me.

The market consisted of displays of food on blankets or roughhewn wooden tables. Bananas, coconuts, potatoes, and beans were plentiful. There were also burlap sacks filled with rice and millet. Scattered between the displays of food were piles of household items like cups, utensils, plastic pails, sponges, and towels. I was looking for a Coke or something to drink, but I couldn't find anything. I also wouldn't mind a granola bar or snack of some kind. There were no packaged foods here. As I reached the end of the displays I discovered that the market continued inside a building. I walked into a dark area that reminded me of the catacombs with narrow, irregularly spaced hallways off of which small bare dark rooms served as the shops of this mall. There was no light except for what came from small openings in the walls up near the ceiling. The layout was strange. You never knew where you would discover a room or another hallway. The air was stuffy and pungent with the smell of fish. I found the source after a couple of more turns. In a large room, set up on plywood tables was a great display of fish. None of the fish were cleaned. They still had their heads. There was no ice. Two women sat in the corner on crates and eyed me flatly when I entered the room. I nodded and smiled.

I found my way out of the caverns and back into the sunlight. So as not to leave empty-handed I bought a cup of yogurt and a banana. The yogurt came in a handmade clay cup that I thought I might have to return, but then it dawned on me that they used clay only because they had no manufactured paper or plastic containers.

I headed back to Baba's house. The guard let me in the compound. My stomach was beginning to feel a little queasy. In the middle of the courtyard, on a small stand, there now stood a large, shiny aluminum pot filled with water. I took off the lid. The water looked clean. I wondered if it was safe. I was really thirsty now. I decided that the monks wouldn't put out bad water knowing that many people would be jeopardized. I took the ladle filled with water and drank every drop. My caution was unwarranted. As it turned out I already had a deadly strain of dysentery circulating in my body.

Dysentery

I found out that in an hour, Baba was going to give his *darshan*. This meant that he would come down to the room in which I had meditated and give a lecture or perhaps a demonstration of some kind. This was more like it. I kicked my shoes off at the door and went inside the room. I grabbed a place along the wall about five people back from the dais. This was going to be great. I was close enough to see every expression on Baba's face. Images of Jamaica suddenly flooded my mind. I felt my heart soften.

After about a half-hour my gut was feeling real bad. I felt like I should get up and walk around but now I didn't dare. The room was filling up rapidly with Indian Margiis. I realized that Baba must give his darshan at this time on a regular basis and people in the neighborhood would stop what they were doing and come over to hear him.

In another fifteen minutes, the pressure in my gut was unbearable. I needed to get to a bathroom bad. I got up and began tiptoeing through the crowd back to the door. By now the crowd was so thick you could barely see an inch of floor space and the process was unbearably slow. By the time I reached the door and pushed my way through a small crowd standing at the entrance I was desperate. I asked people where there was a bathroom, but they all just smiled and nodded. More wasted time. I found the guard by the gate again and asked him where the toilet was. He saw that I was troubled and pointed immediately to a little door near the rear of the house. Thank God it was empty. It was almost pitch black in there though and smelled bad. As I rushed to unzip my pants, I realized that there was no toilet. There was only a hole in the dirt floor with a clay slab on each side of it to stand on. This is why Indian men don't wear pants, I realized. God, I was in major pain now. I felt that I would explode. I kicked off my shoes. Whipped off my pants, pulled up my shirt and squatted over the open hole. I could feel water pour out of me like a faucet.

Needless to say, there was no toilet paper in the room. I did find a pitcher of water though that I used to clean myself.

I was feeling a little better now and I raced to get my pants and shoes back on to hear Baba. Back at the room a crowd of men blocked the back door trying to see over each other. So much for seeing Baba. . . . And then something nice happened. An Indian man turned around to look at me. When he realized I was a foreign visitor he beckoned me to come forward. As I did so, he opened up a path before him and I entered the room. He asked some women who were sitting by the door to make room and enough space was created for me to stand against the wall just inside the door.

I could now see Baba sitting slightly above the solid mass of heads. He looked small and cranky. His gestures were erratic. I could barely make out his voice and when I did I couldn't understand him. He talked on for about forty-five minutes and never cracked a smile. Occasionally the crowd would give out a short laugh or cry or a few people would yell out "Baba!"

At the end of his talk Baba raised his voice as he spoke and the crowd began yelling "Baba, Baba" very intently and then Baba got up abruptly. Someone handed him a cane and he left the room.

There has always been a deep-seated awareness among Margiis about a concept we call "clash." I was beginning to remember about "clash" and it fortified me. The idea was that in order to make spiritual progress you had to experience negativity in like proportion. You had to "burn" through your bad karma, and this was generally painful. Margiis called this negative experience "clash." I remember going on retreats when I was younger. We would feel very high from the intense meditation that we did, but invariably something would go wrong. Our car would break down at night, something like that. So it followed a pattern. The discomfort that I was now feeling was just par for the course.

Outside, in the courtroom I heard a Dada announce that Baba would not be seeing anyone for the rest of the day. Sure, it figures, I thought.

I decided that rather than grousing around I would use every opportunity to purify myself and prepare my mind to meet the Master. There is a saying that goes "when a pickpocket meets the Lord, he sees only his pockets." If Baba really was the Lord, what would I see?

After reading for an hour or so, I meditated again. As I sat there nearing the end of my meditation, I heard people begin to sing "Baba Nam Kevalam" and I realized they were beginning a group meditation. I got up and did kiirtan and then sat down for another meditation. By the time we finished, I had to go to the toilet again. I left the room before the closing prayers in case anybody would beat me to the little room. I didn't know I had dysentery yet, but something was definitely wrong.

Back outside Purusottama told me that a few people were going to go to a restaurant and asked if I would like to join them. I happily said yes having had nothing but stringy yogurt and a banana since I arrived in India.

We walked to the restaurant. It was almost dark by now and as we walked along the side of a road without houses, in the lights of a passing car, we could see the blue fog and smell the acrid scent of Sterno and burning dung.

The restaurant was small but clean, with simple vegetarian food. Afterward, we hailed a cab and had to wait awhile for a second one to come by. Again there was an intense negotiation with a couple of the men. We got into the cabs but the drivers were in bad humor because they wanted more money. The women took one cab back to Tiljala. The men took the second.

The next day we went to Lake Gardens early. There was now another young college guy in my room, so he went with us. This time three of us got into the rickshaw.

When we got to Baba's house, we found Dada Ramananda who was the "in-charge." He was actually Baba's personal secretary. He told us that there was already a list of people who were scheduled to see Baba for the day. He advised us to get there earlier tomorrow. I thought Dada appeared a little jumpy and too preoccupied. I could just imagine how busy Baba must keep him. It was general knowledge how Baba pushed his monks and nuns to work, giving them inhumanly impossible tasks and beating them with his cane when they didn't perform. It was routine for an acharya to be sent to a totally strange country, where he or she in all likelihood could not even speak the language. They'd be given fifty dollars and with no contacts, be told they must start a school or children's home or some other project. It was generally believed that those who held organizational positions around Baba personally went through even greater trials. It was no wonder then that Dada R, who was Baba's personal secretary, would look like a man who spent every moment on red alert. It was the "Clash" principle at work again. Baba would often remind us how obstacles were our friends. The bigger the obstacle, the greater the progress that was possible. Much of the mystery and magic that formed the aura around Baba, especially for new members of Ananda Marga, were the stories told by the monks and nuns about how they found themselves in impossible or even dangerous situations and Baba had miraculously saved them. Everyone that had made a sacrifice to work for Baba's mission had his or her stories to tell. I imagined the stories that Dada R could tell if you could ever get a moment of his time. Many years later, Dada R. published a small book about his experiences with Baba. On the back cover, there was a picture of him in his orange robe and long white beard, with birds resting on his lap and eating out of his hand.

 I broke off from my companions and found a place against the wall to read. After that I meditated. My meditation was disturbed again by an explosive feeling in my gut. Something was definitely wrong. Three times to the toilet before noon and all water. This time when I got out of the little room I began asking if there was a doctor around. There wasn't, but after about an hour or so, one of the men I had asked came up to me with another man who he indicated was a doctor. The man listened to my urgent story with a sublime look on his face and then told me that I should go to a pharmacy and purchase electrolytes. He assured me if I did so, I would be fine. I didn't know what electrolytes were, but I was encouraged by the man's confidence.

 I needed to get to a pharmacy, but I also needed to get some money. I found a Dada who agreed to accompany me on my chores. We took a bus to downtown Calcutta and walked down a crowded little street that cut off from the main drag. We walked into a nondescript building. The wooden floor was worn and dirty. It quickly narrowed into an aisle that ran along a wall that had a single clerk's window in it. This was the bank. There were a couple of men standing in front of the window arguing with the clerk and with another man standing behind the clerk. I was surprised to see that there were no bars on the window.

INSIDE ME, OUTSIDE ME 87

After a minute, the arguing customers left in anger. I stepped up to the window, took two 100-rupee bills out of my wallet and asked the clerk for ten and twenty rupee bills. He looked at me like I was a real pain in the ass. With a scowl, he pulled out a wad of the filthiest, limpest money I had ever seen and began to count the bills. In the US, this stuff would have been taken out of circulation and burned long ago. It gave me the willies to even touch it, but I knew I'd better take it. I paid Dada for the cab ride and we walked out into the street. We went looking for a pharmacy, but couldn't find one. We walked by a jewelry store, airline office, guitar shop, and a place that sold material for saris along with little bronze statues of Buddha, Ganesh, and Shiva, but no drug store. Dada told me that he knew a place back in Lake Gardens that we could go to. That was fine with me.

There was a pharmacy about two blocks from Baba's house. It was cut out of the rear of a building and faced the alley. Basically, it was a room about eight feet wide by four feet deep. Customers could not enter the room because of an imposing counter that ran along the alley. A case of goods from the ceiling to the floor filled the back wall. Two men sat on stools behind the counter. Everything was painted white and it felt clean and safe. The men had clean white shirts on and their black hair was neatly trimmed and combed. I asked for electrolytes and promptly received a green and white box. The box said it was for "dehydration." I didn't have the presence of mind to think that this stuff wasn't going to kill any of the micro-organisms that had invaded my body and was now waging an all-out war inside me. The electrolytes would buy me some time however.

I ordered a bottle of water, but they had run out. We walked a couple of stands down and got a Coke. Coke was always warm in India due to lack of refrigeration. I guzzled a little and then poured the electrolyte powder into the bottle. Mixing the electrolytes with Coke was not one of my brightest ideas. The carbonation exaggerated the constant pressure in my gut and I told Dada that I had to hurry back to Baba's house to use the toilet. I hadn't eaten any food that day. Neither would I eat anything for the rest of the day.

Day Four – The Telephone Bhavan

My fourth day in Calcutta (now called Kolkata) dawned hot and humid like the days preceding it. I was in a rotten mood. I was covered with mosquito bites, feeling sorry for myself, and generally believing that life sucked. Aside from the discomfort of sleeping on a stone floor in just a bag, I was bombarded by mosquitoes that passed at will through the metal grates that served as windows. To avoid the mosquitoes, you had to completely cover yourself in the sleeping bag. But it was impossible to breathe like this and the heat inside the bag would become unbearable. So, you'd kick the covers off in your sleep and the mosquitoes would descend again. Nobody had mosquito netting and it did not dawn on me to buy any. It was a vicious cycle, that left me dazed, grumpy, and in a stupor from sleeplessness.

I stumbled into the washroom and turned on the shower. As the water ran down my hair and over my face a chilling thought came to me. I realized that it was probably the water from this shower that had given me the dysentery. I probably got water in my mouth while I was washing or rinsing my face. It had to be this water, I thought. The only other thing it could have been was the tea I had in the airport in Delhi or the water from the pot that was set up in the courtyard at Lake Gardens. It was unlikely that the tea was to blame because it had been boiled. As for the water at Baba's house, no one else had gotten dysentery. All the rest of the time I had used bottled water, including when I brushed my teeth.

I clamped my lips tight and finished my shower. The first thing I did when I turned off the tap was to rub my lips dry with my towel. Sh*t.

My body was starting to weaken from the dysentery. I had lost my appetite completely and it actually had become uncomfortable to eat. The process of digestion hurt.

I took my time getting myself together for the day. I even wrote some postcards that I had bought at the airport.

The men that I usually traveled with to Lake Garden had left earlier so I was on my own. I decided to stay in my room and meditate. It felt good to be alone. The futility of my attempts to see Baba, Mr. Sarkar, so far was beginning to weigh on me. I felt far from him at this time and I was beginning to doubt my purpose for being here. Aside from seeing him the first day at his darshan, I had only seen him one other time when he came out of his house for a car ride. It was a daily routine for Mr. Sarkar to go for a short ride each afternoon. He only went with his bodyguards, but it was an opportunity for his disciples to see him when he left his house and returned.

I was on the waiting list to see Baba, but I had no idea when that would be. Now I even began to doubt if I would see him before I had to leave. I had heard stories of people who had come to see him and left without having the opportunity to do so. I was now frustrated, confused, sick, and alone. I should have stayed in New York.

After feeling sorry for myself for about an hour, I decided to go to Lake Gardens. I walked to the bypass road and took a bus into the downtown area and from there took a cab to Baba's house. It was about three times as expensive as the normal means of travel and not much faster, but I didn't care.

It was now just before noon. Things looked the same as they usually did. I was lucky to see Dada Ramananda come out of the house as I arrived. I asked him if I was still on the list to see

Baba. He told me that I was. I asked him if I was on the list for the day. He fumbled for a piece of paper and finding it, told me that I was not. I asked him point blank, did he think I would see Baba before I had to leave in two more days? He shrugged his shoulders. I asked him how the names were chosen for the day. He told me that each day Baba told him who he wanted to see on that day.

I wanted to ask Dada if he knew what Baba's decision was based upon, but before I could get out the question Dada excused himself and rushed to talk to someone he saw walking by.

This is just great, I thought. No rhyme or reason to anything. I was on the list, but essentially it didn't mean anything. What was going on here? I began to seriously ponder my situation. Yes, it was insane that I was here. My health was fading fast. My skin was now very dry and becoming hard to the touch. I still had no appetite and I still was running to the toilet seven or eight times a day. My sh*t was totally liquid now and it didn't smell. As soon as I would relieve myself, the pressure in my gut would begin to build again until it would become so great that the liquid would explode out of me. I had better be near a toilet when this happened because I couldn't control myself.

Given this insanity, the possibility still existed that Baba could read my mind, that he knew my innermost thoughts and desires, that he knew everything that I was going through and that everything was moving along for the best, whatever that meant. In short, I was becoming schizophrenic.

I chose to remain positive. I chose to believe that I was just going through clash because something great was still in store for me. I was paying my dues in order to stand in the presence of God.

I prayed, "Dear Lord, I have come from so far away to see you. Please may I see you before I must leave. Time is getting short, my Lord. I believe in you. Please do not forsake me."

I found myself in the big room again and sat down against a wall to meditate. By now meditation was extremely difficult. I couldn't focus my mind. I was in a cloud of pain and stupor. I decided just to sit quietly and repeat my mantra with my eyes open. After doing so for a few minutes, Purusotama walked up and greeted me. He told me that he was going downtown and wanted to know if I cared to come along. I told him that I had been thinking of making a phone call to Ellen since I had arrived in India, but had been unable to because there was no phone in Tiljala or at Baba's house in Lake Gardens. He told me that we should be able to place a call from the Telephone Bhavan (building) that was downtown. "Perfect," I thought.

We walked a couple of blocks to a main road and got a bus. We found the Telephone Bhavan without much trouble. I don't know what I was expecting, but it certainly wasn't the Telephone Bhavan.

Inside the building, out of the bright glare of day, we walked up to a long counter. I told the man that I wanted to make a call to New York City. He gave me a form to fill out that required basic information, including my country of origin. I found a short stubby pencil, filled out the form and gave it back to the man. He looked it over with slow deliberation. Then, he handed me a worn piece of paper and walked away.

Purusottama informed me that I had to give the piece of paper to a man standing behind me. I turned to see a small man in a short-sleeved white shirt standing by a half-door that permitted entrance into a confined space in which there were twenty people or so sitting in pews. They faced a wall which had four telephones on it. Every telephone was being used. The picture became clear immediately. The thing that made me a little anxious was the crowd of guys sitting in the pews. They looked like they had been camped out for days. Dried food plates and scattered newspapers. A couple of guys were even sleeping. It was a hot stuffy room, with a lazy ceiling fan that had no impact on anything. Ten minutes went by. The four original guys were still on the phones. Hmmm.

Purosottama told me that he was going to do an errand. It would take him about a half-hour and it didn't look like I would be finished before then. He had that little glint in his eye that I had come to enjoy. I smiled ruefully at him and nodded.

I took a seat in the front pew, hoping that if I put out a certain anxious, impatient vibe, the kind that often worked in New York, things would move more quickly. I soon realized that once you made it to the phone you could monopolize it as long as you could manage to stand.

These four phones were dedicated to international calls. In the event that you actually got a call through to another country, someone had to answer the phone; you had to have a good connection; you had to dial the right number; etc. In the event that any of these necessities failed, you would dial again and hope for the best. If not, you could wait awhile and try again.

In the forty-five minutes before Purusottama returned only one guy left the phone. At this rate I could expect to get a line out in about twenty hours and then it'd be my luck that Ellen would be out of the apartment. I tried to do the math, let's see, its 1:28 p.m. in Calcutta, so that means it's, what? Twelve hours later ... earlier in New York? So if I call in twenty hours that would be what day in New York? My brain locked up. How the hell could India compete in the global economy? This was a big city, for Christ sake.

I found myself outside on the street shaking my head. Purusottama was staring at me patiently. I was searching my brain for other options. Hey! What about Western Union. Maybe they would have a telegraph office in town.

As luck would have it, the first man we stopped on the street spoke English. He confirmed that there was an office in town, and in fact, the office was only a couple of blocks away.

We followed the man's directions and voila! There was the Western Union sign. Ah, the conveniences of civilization.

Like the other buildings I had been in, it was dark inside, the only light coming from the window and open door. As we entered, we had to squeeze by a small knot of men standing at a counter just inside the door. There were a lot of men standing around talking or filling out forms at shelves around the walls.

It didn't take us long to realize that the action was at the counter. I moved quickly to take my place with the other men and quickly became frustrated that there was no line or queue. It was hard to tell who was first or second. I also felt the anxiety one feels when anyone can come in after you and be served first. I eyed the door warily.

What transpired drove me crazy. The clerk was looking for a message that supposedly had been sent to one of the men. He kept leaving the counter and coming back empty handed. Now the man was becoming obstinate, but the clerk didn't have the juice to dismiss the guy. Instead, in the middle of another exchange with the man, two other men started telling the clerk their business. The clerk drifted from the first guy and began listening to the story of these guys. Now before he could leave the counter another man engaged the clerk and took his attention. The clerk couldn't keep his focus. Before he could complete one task, he would become distracted by a request to perform another, and then in the performance of the second task, he would be pulled to a third, and then the first guy would get upset again and demand the clerk satisfy his need before the others. It was maddening to witness. Soon more people were elbowing to get to the counter and yell at the clerk. The clerk plodded along, never changing his pace or expression. How long could he keep up this insanity? What was even more unbelievable, is that everybody seemed used to the drama, as if this was the normal state of events. I burst into the street gasping for air; my guts now ready to blow out again.

I found a restaurant where I could use the facilities and we went back to Lake Gardens. We arrived just in time to see Baba entering his car for his afternoon ride. He had a crotchety expression on his face again as he gave people his namaskar.

I desperately needed some sweetness. I couldn't find any. Life was becoming surreal. I only had one more day in India and I was seriously breaking down. I watched Baba's car drive through the gate and move down the alley. I decided to go back to Tiljala.

Day Six

I had dropped almost fifteen pounds and was looking gaunt. My skin felt like wood. I wanted to get to Baba's house as early as I could. I must see him before leaving India and my flight was scheduled for tomorrow afternoon.

I rose early, but rather than travel alone in my condition, I decided to wait and travel with others. I was impatient and didn't speak to anyone once we got on the road. There were five of us now, having been joined by two other American young men who I didn't know, nor cared to get to know. My mood dampened everyone's spirits and Purusottama was looking more concerned about me than usual. When we arrived at Baba's house, it was the same story. Baba had announced seven or eight people that he wanted to see that day and I wasn't one of them. I became immediately depressed. This is bullshit, I thought. My mind was at war. Believe or disbelieve, accept or denounce. I went into the big room and tried to meditate. It was useless. My mind was swimming in a raging confusion. I felt cold. I began looking around the room for a blanket to cover myself. I grabbed someone's meditation blanket and struggled to get it over my shoulders. I sat huddled against the wall with my legs drawn up to my chest and my head on my knees.

I sat there for some time, drifting in and out of consciousness. What should I do? What if Baba won't see me? What if I have to go back without seeing him? The little flower of hope that I had planted in my heart was now being ripped apart by a black storm of doubt and confusion. I felt like crying, but my anger held back the tears. Maybe I should get to a hospital. I was surprised that this thought had not come to me before. If I was back in New York, I would have gone to an Emergency Room days ago. For some reason, I still could not get myself to budge. Maybe it was fear of the unknown. Maybe I didn't trust Indian hospitals to make me well. Maybe I was afraid of the cost or not having medical coverage in India. As I sorted through these possibilities, I realized that none of these reasons were holding me back. What kept me from seeking out a hospital was the belief that my illness was part of a spiritual cleansing and that if Baba wanted to, he could completely cure me with a snap of his fingers. He had cured so many others, if the stories were to be believed; why couldn't he cure me? In my state of mind, I couldn't tell if I was being pathetic or I was right on target.

At some point, my friend Purusottama came up to me. He had brought an Indian Dada with him and they squatted down to look at me.

"Citsvarup," he said, using my Ananda Marga name, "some Dadas have an apartment not too far from here. Maybe it would be a good idea for you to go over there and get a little rest. If you want to go, this Dada will take you there."

"This is my last day to see Baba," I said, "what if he wants to see me?"

The monk replied that someone would come and get me.

Under the circumstances it seemed like a good offer. The men helped me up. Outside on the street, Dada negotiated with one of the rickshaw drivers who were waiting nearby. I took the blanket with me because I was still cold. I hoped it would be okay. The ride to the apartment took us deeper into the residential area. As we moved along, I tried to remember the way, but it was useless. There were no street signs. There were no stop signs. There were no blocks. Often there were no corners. The ride just snaked along through curves and half blocks, through streets that often seemed like alleys, dense with people, with every blade of grass or plant stomped to death long ago. I prayed that someone would be at the house to accompany me back to Baba's when it was time to return.

We finally arrived at another nondescript brick building. It looked clean, however, well built, and safe. The outside door and the apartment door required a key to open them.

The apartment was up one flight of stairs. The door opened onto a large room with absolutely nothing in it. The floor was concrete and there were cabinets built into the wall on the right. A narrow counter ran under the cabinets but nothing was on it. Neither was there anything on the walls. The room and cabinets were painted maintenance room gray. I never saw a space that could have used a woman's touch more than this one. Something else struck me about this room. If this was supposed to be a kitchen, there was no refrigerator, nor stove, nor kitchen sink to be seen.

While I puzzled over this strange phenomenon, I spotted the bathroom at the far end of the "kitchen" and excused myself.

I knew what a bathroom looked like by now. This one consisted of a hole in the floor and a spigot beside it that came out of the wall at kneecap height. A plastic bucket sat under the spigot filled with water. Another little plastic pitcher floated on top of the water. There was a square lip of concrete about two inches high that ran around the spigot area to keep the water from flowing onto the rest of the floor. In this area one would squat and pour water over one's head with the little pitcher. The little pitcher was also used to clean oneself after using the hole in the floor. It was a simple system that did not require Dove soap, Revlon shampoo, towels, towel racks, wash cloths, a medicine cabinet, hooks, shower curtains, mirrors, throw rugs, or anything else that I felt was indispensable in a bathroom. It didn't even require a toilet or a shower stall. I felt a pang of admiration for its simplicity. I was still cussing the fact, however, that I had to remove my shoes, socks pants and underwear every time I needed to use one of these holes in the floor. If I had any sense whatsoever, I would have replaced my western clothes with a dhoti and lungi long ago. Amazingly, the thought had never even crossed my mind, so strong was my cultural bias.

Dada introduced me to another monk and two initiates who all slept in one room. There was another man who slept in their room, but he was not present.

There was another smaller bedroom off the kitchen just to the right as you entered the apartment. Three more men slept in this room.

It was now about 10:00 a.m. and I was very tired. Dada took me into the larger bedroom. It consisted of four sleeping stations. Each "bed" was simply a blanket doubled over. Between the beds there were a couple of objects like books, or pictures of Baba. There was a closet with a couple of shirts hanging in it. So much for material possessions.

Dada pointed to one of the blankets on the floor and told me that I could sleep there because the brother whose bed that was would not be returning for the day. I thanked Dada and lay down immediately. The room was full of light and it was very hot. A ceiling fan in the kitchen pulled air through the open windows, but you couldn't feel anything. Actually, I was glad about this because I was feeling cold. I remember turning over and seeing one of the young men standing over me with a blanket. He covered me with it, smiled at me, and left the room, drawing the door closed to cut out the noise from the conversations going on in the kitchen.

It was a simple act of kindness from a stranger, but it made me feel safe. It took a lot of tension out of me and I fell asleep almost immediately.

I awoke a couple of hours later to a commotion in the kitchen. The bedroom door was open a crack and I could see men moving back and forth. I got up to take a closer look.

It was a kitchen after all. Seven men squatted around a pot and a wok on the floor. The pot was filled with water. The wok had cooking oil in it. Tins of Sterno burned under both. Four or five men were busily chopping vegetables on cutting boards as they squatted on the floor. Green beans, eggplant, carrots, and potatoes went into the wok as they were cut. When the water in the second pot started to boil, rice from a paper bag was poured into it and covered. Because the men who were cutting vegetables were also taking them from paper bags, I realized that they must buy food for each meal.

One Dada stirred the vegetables, adding some spices as he worked. Soon the meal was ready. Everyone kept their same places as a young man filled a stack of aluminum plates with food and passed them around. I was offered a plate but declined. The idea of eating food was beyond me at this point. I had no appetite and I couldn't imagine what a plate of rice and vegetables would do to me. I was also offered a plastic cup with lemon water, but I declined this too.

The men ate in silence except for small comments now and then. Even so, the mood was congenial.

Just as quickly and methodically as the meal had come together it was disassembled. Plates, cups, and utensils were cleaned, dried and put on shelves in the cabinet. The Sterno tins were put out, the floor was swept, and presto the room was completely empty again. Everyone exited the apartment except for one Dada who went back to work in a tiny office space off the second bedroom. I was left standing there in silence. The whole meal had not taken much longer than a half hour. I went back to bed.

I awoke about four thirty in the afternoon feeling achy and wanting to return to Baba's house. Perhaps, by some miracle, Baba would see me.

I found Dada sitting in his office and asked if someone could take me back to Baba's.

"No," he said. "People will not be returning for another hour or two. Perhaps you can wait." I didn't want to wait and yet in remembering the labyrinth that I had come through to get here, I wasn't excited about traveling by myself either.

Dada saw my consternation and assured me that if I wanted to go now, it would not be a problem.

"Come", he said, "I will help you get a cab." I was feeling very vulnerable, but I followed Dada outside. We stood on a curb and waited. There was not a lot of traffic, nor were there many people in sight. The smell of cow dung and Sterno still hung in the dead air and made me feel sick to my stomach.

Soon a rickshaw came by. Dada waved it down and negotiated with the driver. He paid the man out of his own pocket. I thanked Dada, gave him my Namaskar and we took off.

I rode uneasily through the neighborhood streets and went on red alert on one occasion when the "driver" stopped to speak to a couple of men who waved to him from the side of the street. I couldn't understand a word they were saying, but I watched their faces intently for any sign of hostility or scheming. Nothing happened and we were soon on our way again.

Without further incident we arrived at Baba's house. As I got out of the rickshaw and walked to the gate, the man started speaking to me in an angry voice. A man standing nearby told me that the driver was demanding another rupee. Figuring that Dada had cut a strict deal, I gave the guy his rupee and still scowling he turned his rickshaw around and left.

Nothing more happened that night. I took a cab back to Tiljala with a Didi and an older Indian woman and went to bed without meditating.

Day Seven

The day dawned full of anxiety and trepidation. My plane was leaving at 5:30 p.m. this evening. What if Baba wouldn't see me? The possibility was now very real. I dreaded going to Baba's to discover that I wasn't on the "list." I felt taken advantage of. I felt betrayed, but another part of me denounced my wimpiness. This was the path of Tantra. The path of a warrior. How many times did I need to remind myself that in order to make spiritual progress, I had to face the pain of reality like a warrior. This was the way of internal purification. Mine was a warrior's path and this was the gauntlet. Why couldn't I understand this? Why couldn't I accept it?

"Right", I told myself. "If it's meant to be, then Baba will see me, if not so be it."

I got dressed, rolled up my sleeping bag and packed my belongings. I decided that I would leave my bags here rather than take them to Lake Gardens. I could take a cab back here and then head to the airport.

When I arrived at Lake Gardens, I was immediately struck by how similar my arrival was to that of previous days. It instantly felt bad. I began to look for Dada Ramananda, but a sour burn began to fill my gut. It wasn't dysentery. It was frustration, anger, and God knows what else. How could Baba do this to me? Then I began to think that maybe he wasn't doing anything.

Maybe this whole thing was just a lot of hype. I walked to the meditation room, but couldn't go in. I was seeing red. F*ck this sh*t. I paced around the compound. I walked into the garden and found a little solitude. I began to come unglued. God, what the hell do you want from me? I have come thousands of miles to see you. I've gotten deadly sick. My skin's like wood. I can hardly see my eyes in the black caverns of my eye sockets. I've jeopardized everything. For what!? Now hot tears flowed down my cheeks. My brain was melting down. All hail to schizophrenia! One half of my brain defended my reality as being exactly what it should be and condemned my behavior as unacceptable. The other side of my brain railed against the injustice of my situation and told me to leave this hell hole immediately if I wanted to get back home alive.

The contradiction that had been brewing in my thoughts for days was now erupting like a cancerous boil. I felt the heat being generated in my head. Sweat soaked my hair and face.

It was unbearable. One minute I would beg God to help me understand what was going on. "Please see me Baba. Please." The next moment I would venomously condemn myself for my pitiable begging. "What kind of a man are you anyway? I am a professional," I would tell myself. "I own a business on Fifth Avenue in New York. I'm a success. I don't need this sh*t."

My mind heaved from side to side. Maddening, unstoppable, brave, outraged, pathetic, rational, stubborn, wise, and whimpering, incapable of knowing what to feel or what to believe.

I don't know how long I remained in this state. I remember going to the toilet a couple of more times. I remember pacing in the alley. I remember sitting on the little bench outside the meditation room. And then something totally out of the blue occurred.

As I raised my head, I saw an old woman, with white hair, wearing a long blue sari, standing before me. She was flanked by nuns in orange who supported her. I recognized the woman at once. It was Jane Benzel, an old friend from Carbondale. It was a shock and a blessing to see her. I felt that a guardian angel had descended. As I stood up to give her a hug, a look of horror crossed the faces of the nuns and they pulled Jane back from me.

I realized then that I must really look a sight to frighten them so. I stopped, but Jane motioned to the nuns to release her and with her bright blue eyes brighter than ever and happy as a clam, she gave me a big hug. I struggled to gain my composure.

When I was a student in Carbondale, freshly initiated into the Ananda Marga yoga practices, Jane was a local hairdresser on the verge of retirement. We got to know each other through our weekly group meditations. She was originally from Kentucky, had a down-home manner, an easy laugh, and a light spirit than no one ever saw turn bad.

It's not that it was all roses for Jane. Her husband was a pathetic alcoholic, with a fascination for guns, who bad-mouthed her relentlessly for her association with Ananda Marga. She spent a lot of time taking care of him and got only grief in return. Nonetheless, no one ever suspected she had a care in the world.

Jane was a modern-day saint, we figured. For her, everything came from God, good or bad. It was there for her to learn from and enjoy.

Jane had never seen me in a bad way before and I was somewhat embarrassed to see her now. Yet, when I looked into her eyes, I saw the same intense understanding that I always remembered.

We sat down on the little bench together and I told Jane my story. She listened quietly as I related how I had gotten dysentery, how Baba would not see me, and how my mind was breaking down.

When I finished my story, Jane just sat there looking intently into my eyes. She then asked me when my plane was leaving. I told her it would leave in about five hours.

As I said this, she closed her eyes and remained quiet for several minutes. When she opened her eyes again, she turned to me with a big grin on her face and said "Honey, I know everything is going to work out just fine. I know you'll make the right decision. I just know that you will."

It was one of those moments in time when reality crystallizes into a single thought. By this simple sentence it was as if a complex code had been broken. As ridiculous as it sounds, I realized that all the obsessive convolutions of my mind, the confusion and pain, came down to my not making a simple decision. It all came down to *deciding* whether I should stay or go. No one else could make this decision for me. Not even Baba.

Jane watched me and told me she was going inside to meditate. I helped her stand up. She winked and walked off. When Jane left, I closed my eyes and saw immediately what I must do. I had forgotten an important tenet of Tantric practice—surrender to the Guru. I had come here in my New York "Yankee" mindset. It said "I'm a busy and important man. I've committed a week's time to determine if my master is God-realized. He has a week to prove himself to me and then I need to go back to work." I hadn't thought much about what it would be like if I found out that he was self-realized or indeed, how he would prove it to me. I just thought I would be able to go back to New York secure in the fact that there was a God, that He existed in the form of man, and I had met Him. I supposed this would be plenty. I had the mentality of a vacation brochure. Yes, I visited the Rocky Mountains. They were awesome. I could say that I've been there and done that.

What did it mean to surrender to the Guru? My mind wrestled with this question. One surrenders to a spiritual master because if you feel in your heart that someone is a master, he would know the way to get to God better than you. It's just like studying with a karate master. In time you might be able to teach yourself karate by reading books and watching videotapes, but it is not the same as studying with a master who understands your every move and can correct it as it occurs. It's like that with a spiritual master too, but infinitely more complicated. While the karate master deals in objective reality, the spiritual master deals in subjective reality. The "I-feeling." Where does it begin and where does it end? What is it? Why am I so attached to it? Who am I that is so attached to it?

One surrenders to the Tantric master because he or she knows how *not* to get lost in the mind and how to come out the other side. I thought then about how Baba had given us concrete instructions on how to concentrate through the mind. He has taught us about the nature of consciousness and how the mind is formed. He had explained its link to matter, and how one can overcome its attraction to matter, and in so doing become its master.

When one goes deep within and comes out the other side, "inside me" and "outside me" cease to exist. One enters the Oneness of consciousness. But how do you do this and keep your mind from going crazy?

I reflected on my present state. I was definitely lost in my mind. I understood how to make a living in New York City and though I thought I understood about the spiritual path, I was lost, seriously lost, and I couldn't find my way out.

I gritted my teeth and decided to stay in India. I was going to miss my plane. It didn't matter. In all probability I was going to die here in Calcutta, the armpit of the world. It didn't matter.

My spiritual theory was coming back to me. If matter comes from spirit, as spiritual theory holds, then spirit determines the course of events and not vice-versa. If I surrendered to spirit everything would follow the flow of God's mind. In contrast, if I returned to New York and gave up the trial by fire, I would be a quitter. I would be demoralized and adrift. I would have turned my back on my true self. These were the thoughts that formed in the nucleus of my being and fought back the drenching panic of my body.

"Blessed Father, thy will be done. I am yours to do with as you want. Fill me with your love or kill me. Heaven or hell, it doesn't matter. I am coming for you." I repeated these words over and over in my mind until I heard them like a distant lullaby. A calmness came over me. I looked up at the people moving about the courtyard and they looked calmer too. I felt a little at home for the first time since I arrived a week ago.

Just as I was beginning to enjoy this feeling, a stab of anxiety shot through me. A practical concern. My plane ticket. I was scheduled to fly out of Calcutta in a few hours. I would need to change my flight date or risk losing my ticket altogether, which, if I did, would probably cost me an additional two thousand dollars to order a one-way ticket to the States to replace it. Maybe Baba would take care of this too? Not likely.

As with everything in India, accomplishing this seemed like an insurmountable task. There was no telephone in Baba's house. Where could I find a phone? How would I get the number of the airline? What would I say? For some reason, I didn't despair.

I walked over to a monk and nun talking together and told them my situation. The Dada informed me that Air India had an office in downtown Calcutta and that I would have to go there. I should take my ticket and passport and be prepared to face opposition. I needed to tell them a good reason why I had to stay. "Unfortunately," he added, "seeing your Guru will probably not count as a reason."

As luck would have it, or perhaps I should say, by God's Grace, Dada remembered that another man also had to go to the airline office. He pointed him out to me. I approached the man and told him I was going to the Air India office, would he like to join me. He said that he had his three year old daughter with him and his wife had not yet arrived from the hotel. He said that he had planned on going tomorrow. He apologized seeing my condition, but told me where the office was and how to get there.

Okay, I thought, so what if I have to travel in Calcutta by myself for the first time, in my state, and negotiate a business transaction. I quelled the anxiety beginning in my gut. "I can do this," I thought. "This is what I am supposed to do. Let's do it."

I found Jane sitting in the meditation room and I told her my plan and she laughed. "I knew you'd make the right decision," she said, with her typically exaggerated "my hero" tone to her voice. It was classic Jane. I could never figure out if she was overly spacey or just filled with mocking delight. In any case, she never ceased to make me feel good.

The man I had talked to told me a cheap way to get to the Air India office, but I was in no mood for rickshaws and buses. I walked to the gate and asked the guard to let me out. As I did so, the same man called out for me to wait. He had found someone to keep an eye on his little girl and would like to join me. "Terrific."

The Air India office was professional by western standards. There were carpets on the floor and comfortable chairs beside the agents' desks. The place was air-conditioned. This really brought home what I had been missing in the hot swarmy nights in Tiljala.

I sat down beside the desk of a proper Indian woman with slicked back hair held tight with a large barrette. I told her that my business required me to stay a few more days and that I needed to reschedule my return flight. She eyed me wearily.

"May I see your passport and ticket," she said.

"Certainly."

She looked at my passport, reading it carefully. She then picked up the ticket and deliberately studied it.

"And what is the reason you must reschedule?" she inquired, now looking steadily into my eyes.

From what Dada had told me, this was the deciding moment. I could lose a couple of thousand dollars here. I became nervous and began to speak in an irritated tone. I told her that I was a buyer from a department store in New York City. I'm here to approve a shipment of clothing back to the US, but the local manufacturer has not yet completed the order.

"My company will not authorize shipment without my final inspection."

She was quiet but continued to appraise me.

"When will the goods be ready?" she said.

"I don't know, three days, four days, five days. They have had difficulty with a couple of their sewing machines."

"Oh?" she raised her eyebrows and shook her head.

"I will need an open return," I said immediately.

It didn't seem like she believed me, but she didn't know what to do. My appearance confused her and complicated the matter in her mind.

"Very well," she concluded and punched something into the computer on her desk.

"When you are ready to return you can come back to this office or go to the ticket counter at the airport. In either case, call ahead when you know your departure date. Unless you do so, you may not get the flight you desire."

I thanked her for her efforts on my behalf. She nodded, but did not smile.

Arjuna, my traveling partner, was still sitting at the other desk talking with an agent. I was too hyper to be in that office a second longer, even if it was air-conditioned. I motioned to him that I would wait outside and he nodded back. A paranoia ran through me that I should not be associated with him in the minds of the agents.

Arjuna was wearing Berkshire sandals, a tee shirt, and loose-fitting yoga pants with a drawstring. I kept thinking that my agent would put two and two together and ask me for a business card, or some proof to verify my story.

Once outside the heat blasted me again. But as I squinted into the hot sun, I was happy. I had achieved the near impossible in one of the weakest moments of my life.

When Arjuna and I returned to Lake Gardens, Baba was just walking out of the house to get in his car for his afternoon ride. People had surrounded the car three or four deep. Two uniformed guards walked at Baba's side, slowly making a path through the crowd so that Baba could get into the car. Arjuna and I were on the street outside the gate peering in. I felt like an orphan looking into a party of a rich and powerful celebrity.

I could see Baba's head moving slowly on the other side of the car. I could see one of the guards opening the rear door on Baba's side of the car. He must have performed this simple action a hundred times. Baba would get into the back seat, the guard would close the door, and hold people back on his side until the car could drive away.

As this little scene played itself out, the man at the gate was telling Arjuna and me to move back so that he could open it to let the car out. We stepped back and waited for the gate to swing open onto the street. It took more effort than simply opening the little door in the gate through which people entered and exited.

As the gate swung passed us, I stepped forward again to see what was going on. Suddenly there was Baba standing a couple feet away looking right at me. He had not gotten into the back seat after all. He had come to the front of the car to see me. I stared at him in utter amazement. The harshness in his face was gone. His face was filled with sweetness and he was looking right at me. There was no mistake about it. He was standing there looking at me. No one else. Nothing else. Just me.

As I stood there gawking at him, he raised his folded hands to his forehead and then to his heart and then he bowed to me. I returned the greeting and he smiled brightly at me.

He then walked back to the open car door, got inside, and the car slowly pulled away from the throng of people, many of whom continued to shout out his name.

I couldn't say a word. I could only think that Baba was aware of me. He must have known all along what I had been going through. He must have been aware of my choice to stay! I could hardly believe it. It seemed an unmistakable sign. Was it unmistakable? Yes, it was! The shell around my heart cracked open and I could breathe much easier.

As I stood there in my reverie, Jane came up beside me. She wanted to know if I had seen what had happened. I felt that Jane had come along at just the right moment to help me blast through my schizophrenia. She was a gift of God. I smiled at her through my tears. And she smiled back at me through hers.

The next morning when I arrived at Lake Gardens, I was told that Baba would see me today. I immediately knew that my decision to surrender to Baba was a correct one. How else could the Guru expand my consciousness beyond the limited scope of my ego, unless I gave him permission to do so? It seemed so clear now. "Not my will but Thine be done, Oh Lord." How many religions have this as one of their tenets, if not all?

"But was Baba God?" Just the sound of the question in my mind, made me gasp. I wanted to believe with every fiber of my being now, but I still didn't know. I only knew that he was not like any mortal I had ever met. He was beyond the sphere of mortal accomplishments. He was something unfathomable and capable of a love that made me weep. At the same time, he could be a harsh task master.

I was told to wait in the darshan room and that I would be called when the time came. I did not have long to wait. A monk rushed into the room after about forty-five minutes and looked around nervously.

"Citsvarup. Where is Citsvarup?!"

"I am here Dada," I said.

"Come, come," he said hurriedly.

I followed him through a door that he immediately closed behind us. I found myself facing a carpeted staircase that went up about five or six steps to a small landing and then cut back for another five or six steps. When I reached the landing, I saw four people sitting on the steps above me, waiting in line. Dada pointed at the step closest to me and told me to sit and wait. He immediately went up the stairs and disappeared into a room at the top.

After ten minutes or so the door directly facing the staircase opened and a man came out. He closed the door reverentially behind him. I knew at once this must be Baba's room. Dada came out of his room hurriedly and motioned for the man on the top step to go in.

"Quickly, quickly," he admonished.

Dada opened the door to Baba's room and the man went in. Dada pulled the door closed behind him. Now only three people were sitting between me and Baba.

I began to feel the significance of my situation. I was about to come face to face with a spiritual master, perhaps a perfect master—one who had by all accounts demonstrated the eight powers of God.[2] Moreover,

---

2 Although Baba never made a public exhibition of his powers (siddhis), he demonstrated them in his darshans to his disciples to illustrate the nature and boundaries of knowledge. The powers are: 1) *Anima*, the ability to transform one's consciousness into each and every physical particle, 2) *Mahima*, the ability to expand the mind to encompass the entire universe, 3) *Laghima*, to make the mind free from any bondage, 4) *Prapti* to attain and to help others attain the Supreme, 5) *Iishitva* to correctly guide others in their physical and psychic progress, 6) *Vashitva* to control and properly regulate everything for the welfare of all, 7) *Prakamya* to

he was *my* spiritual master. I was in my father's house. I began to feel at home. I looked around me. On the walls hung primitive drawings of fish and the Pratik symbol of Ananda Marga.

My breathing became deeper, calmer. I was finally home. I had made it home after a long journey. How long had it been since I was home? I don't know. Possibly lifetimes. It felt like eons since I saw my father last. Whenever it was, it didn't matter. Nothing could stop me from seeing Baba now. Nothing inside me wanted to call him Mr. Sarkar any longer. Baba was much bigger than Mr. Sarkar. He was my spiritual father and I was his son.

Dada came out of his room and began talking to the men in front of me. He asked them what was their posting in the Ananda Marga organization and what duties they had performed. They reported in turn. One was a Unit Secretary[3] in Germany. Another man administered an Ananda Marga school. I can't remember what the third man said.

Then Dada turned to me. "What is your posting?" he inquired.

Because I had not been active in the organization for many years, I had no job title or responsibilities and told Dada so. He immediately became agitated.

"You are not doing organizational work? Are you a Margi?" he challenged.

"Dada, I have not been active in Ananda Marga for a few years. I . . . ."

"Then what are you doing here?" he interrupted. ". . . Baba will not see anyone who has not been working for His mission," he said resolutely.

accomplish whatever one desires, 8) *Antaryamitva* to enter the ectoplasmic and endoplasmic structure of others and know their pain and pleasures.

3   A unit was a community of Ananda Marga members (Margiis) who performed their spiritual practice and service together. A jagriti was their place of worship. The Unit Secretary was the principal organizer.

I did not say anything. I did not panic. I thought this was just another test by the Guru to see if I had faith in him.

Dada was becoming angry.

"You are wasting everyone's time!" he snapped.

"Perhaps Baba will make an exception and see me," I said humbly.

This made him even angrier. He glared at me. Then his face softened into worry. "Wait here," he commanded and rushed up the stairs to his room again.

I looked at the three men above me. They looked at me. No one knew what to make of the situation.

After a few more minutes the door to Baba's room opened again and the next man came out. Dada was there again to hurry the next man in and close the door behind him. He then came down the stairs and sat beside me.

"Where do you live?" he asked annoyed.

"I live in New York City, Dada."

"Okay . . . okay. This is what you are to tell Baba when He asks you about your posting. You are a *bhukti pradhan (Unit Secretary)* in Boston Region. Will you remember?"

I remembered the term bhuki pradhan. It was the person who was responsible for all projects in a local area. It was a role played by a local person and not a monk or nun.

"If I live in New York City, why don't I just say I'm a bhukti pradhan from New York City?" I asked Dada.

Dada's fuse was short.

"New York City is in New York Sector. New York City is in Boston Region which is a region in New York Sector. It is bigger than New York City."

I pondered this while Dada cautioned me that I must get my nominal posting correct otherwise we would both be in serious trouble. A part of me was thinking how preposterous the whole thing was that a monk should be coaching me in a lie to our Guru who had the power to read our minds anyway. He would know what was going on whether we said anything or not. I didn't tell this to Dada who was a jumpy guy. This kind of disrespect for process might put him off the charts. I knew that Dada had his rules to follow and he was trying his best to help me out. I told Dada that I would remember what he told me, but he still looked worried. He went up to his room again.

I looked sheepishly at the two men above me. They looked back at me and smiled.

We sat there in silence for a few minutes when Dada came rushing out of his room again. Oh, no, I thought, what now.

"Citsvarup, are you wearing your Pratik?"

He had the intensity of a drill sergeant.

I couldn't believe it. I had forgotten to wear the symbol of Ananda Marga around my neck. I had worn the medallion for years, like all Margiis, but had not done so for a long time, simply forgetting the practice.

"No Dada, I don't have a Pratik," I said sheepishly.

His mouth dropped and his chest sank in disbelief. Then he asked.

"You are wearing a lungota?"

Now I felt terrible. I was so out of touch with the most basic protocols of my organization. A lungota was a T-shaped piece of cloth that Indian men wore around their private parts. It kept everything nice and tight and, now it occurred to me, was the practical underwear for using the "hole in the floor" toilets in India. Wearing a lungota was also considered a spiritual practice because it reduced sexual stimulation and therefore improved meditation.

"I'm sorry Dada, I am not wearing a lungota," I said dejectedly.

Now Dada was in real pain. I could see that he was wavering about letting me see Baba. I had abandoned the organization years ago, and couldn't even adhere to the simplest protocols. My own confidence was shaken now. Dread entered my intestines again. What if I don't get to see Baba after all this?

I sat there looking forlornly at Dada, believing that he would be in the right if he dismissed me until I could get my act together. If so, who knows when or if Baba would see me again.

Suddenly, Dada's expression changed again. He ran into his office and came out again quickly with a small silver Pratik that hung on a loop of red string. I immediately put it over my head and folded my hands in namaskar to show my heartfelt appreciation. Now he ran down the stairs and did not return.

The door to Baba's room opened and the man came out and walked down the stairs passed me. The next man at the top of the stairs looked warily about, hesitant to enter Baba's room without Dada. But he got up his courage, and went into Baba's room closing the door behind him. I wondered if Baba knew what was going on. Of course, he must. I wondered what he would do to me.

After ten minutes or so Dada had not returned. The door to Baba's room opened again and the last man in front of me entered Baba's room. I was now alone and very nervous. What if Dada didn't return? Should I go into Baba's room anyway? Would it be sacrilegious? I prayed that Dada return.

After about five minutes more, Dada bounded up the stairs and handed me a ball of orange cloth. He motioned for me to go into his office and put it on quickly. As I fumbled getting my pants off and tying the lungota, and getting it fitted, I hoped the door to Baba's room would not open too soon. I didn't want to keep Baba waiting. I also didn't want to meet my spiritual master after so many years, all flustered and straightening my underwear.

By His Grace, I got myself organized, wadded up my BVDs and stuck them into my pants pocket. I sat down on the top stair and closed my eyes to center myself. When I opened my eyes, I looked down at three more men[4] whom Dada had let into the stairwell. Suddenly the door opened and the last man before me walked out. This was it. The moment of truth.

"Go, go," Dada chided, "Don't keep Baba waiting." I smiled at Dada and he smiled back at me. I walked into Baba's room and Dada closed the door behind me.

At The Master's Feet

I looked up and there was Baba all by himself.

He was sitting cross-legged on a small platform that was raised about a foot off the floor. He was dressed in a long white shirt (dhoti) and a white baggy lungi. He looked clean and crisp and friendly. He wore his thick black-framed glasses.

As I stood staring at him, I realized that, as a disciple, I should do *satsang pranam,* which is to prostrate myself at his feet. I did so immediately, having no ego reaction, only feeling the hardness of the bare wooden floor.

Baba motioned for me to get up. I did so and stood before him. I was extremely happy to be there. I felt now that I had my father all to myself. My heart was wide-open.

"And what is your posting, my son?" Baba immediately asked.

"I'm a bhukti pradhan, Baba," I said, following my prompting by Dada.

---

4   Only men were allowed to see Baba in private, so as to defer any criticism of impropriety. When Baba saw women he saw them in small groups.

"Ah very good," Baba said "and what sector are you from?"

"Uh, I am from New York Sector, Baba"

"Ah, New York" Baba nodded approvingly. "And what region do you work in?"

"Uh …." Oh no. I forgot what Dada had told me. If I didn't get the region right Baba would know that I was lying about the posting. A bhukti pradhan would certainly know what region he or she worked in.

"I'm from New York Region, Baba, I said, unable to stall any longer.

It was the wrong answer.

"New York region?" Baba repeated, looking puzzled.

As I looked at him pondering my answer, I knew that he was yanking my chain. He had been aware of the drama that I had been through outside his room. It tickled me. I was very happy to see him. I couldn't take my eyes off him. Nothing in the world mattered now. I was his.

Baba looked up at me with a kind and happy smile. With a little nod, he motioned for me to sit down in front of him. When I did so, I was only about eighteen inches from him. I stared into his dark brown eyes, made huge by the thick glasses that he wore. Baba's appearance was enigmatic. Sometimes he looked like he was seventy or eighty years old. Now he looked like he was in his late forties. Strong and alert.

I basked in Baba's attention. It was like being in the presence of ET—grand, loving, outrageous, mysterious, not to be believed. Baba sat there smiling at me and a warm glow pervaded me. I completely forgot that I was sick. As I took in the love of my father, the scene in the staircase reentered my mind followed immediately by much darker thoughts. Things that I was ashamed to tell anyone—things that made me unworthy to be sitting at a spiritual master's feet.

The thoughts took over my mind, killing my joy. As I looked at Baba, I was suddenly shocked to realize that each of my negative thoughts was also registering in Baba's eyes at the exact moment they crossed my mind. He was reading my mind. I was certain that he was reading my mind!

This realization stopped the flow of my thoughts and I stared into Baba's face waiting to see what he would do now. He had just seen the worst of me. It was such a strange experience. Almost like I was looking into a mirror but instead of seeing my face, I was seeing my mind.

Baba shook his head slowly up and down. "It is true," he said. "You have been a bad boy." Now he waited for me to respond. I didn't know what to say. I felt like a child with his hand caught in the proverbial cookie jar. His demeanor wasn't harsh or condemning.

"Do you think you should be punished?" he asked nonchalantly.

For some reason, this struck my funny bone. I had traveled half way around the world to see Baba and was almost dead from the effort and he wanted to know if I wanted more punishment. All I could think of was, "I really love you Baba." The drama of reality was the thinnest curtain now and I could see right through it. I could reach out and tear it down with the least effort of my fingertips.

I had a smile on my face and I noticed that Baba was smiling the exact smile that I was smiling. Somehow he made the same shape and expression of my lips. God, how could he do that?

"Whatever you think is best, Baba" I said, knowing in my soul that whatever he did would be the perfect solution.

"Put up your arms," he instructed me.

I raised my hands above my head and as I did so Baba pulled out a conductor's wand from behind his back and tapped me lightly on my left rib cage. Then he told me to put my arms down. As I did so, before I knew what was happening, Baba gave me a big hug.

Holding me tightly he repeated over and over "Oh my boy, my boy." He rubbed my back and my head. He squeezed my cheeks like I was a baby. "Ooh, ooh" he said. My eyes gushed with tears. I had made it home again. I was home again. My father loved me. I couldn't believe he really loved me so much. It was everything that I dared to dream of. Bliss shot through me as he rubbed my back, just as it had in Jamaica so many years before.

I could have stayed in Baba's arms forever. I was safe, content, and happy like a child who never experienced anything bad in life. When Baba took his arms from me I still felt that they remained around me. This love he gave me was mine to keep. I could take it anywhere now. I could go to hell itself and be okay. I could go back to New York and be okay.

"I love you Baba", I said, "I love you."

Baba sat there looking at me for a little time and then said,

"I want you to take an oath to be an ideal human being."

I told him that I would do it. He spoke the words of the oath and I repeated them. Then he told me that it was time for me to leave. I had no hesitation. I was filled to the brim.

As I reached for the door, Baba asked me

"My son, will you do great things for humanity?"

I looked back at Baba thinking that only he would ever ask me such a question.

"I'll try Baba," I said.

"No, my son," Baba replied, "you *will* do great things for humanity. You will do very great things."

He smiled brightly and folded his hands in namaskar. I returned the gesture, looking at Baba for one last moment and then left his room.

I would never see Baba in his body again. I came to realize, however, in the remainder of my journey that Baba is more than a man. Baba is a Divine experience. He could exist inside me or outside me. In his body or outside his body. This realization, learned from my experiences that happened next, is perhaps the greatest miracle of all.

Baba as Spirit

Meeting Baba in a body was one thing, but coming to know him outside of his body was still to come. Here is what happened to me on my way back to New York.

When I left Baba's room, I knew that I had to get back to New York immediately. Physically I was close to dying. I hadn't brought my bags from Tiljala that morning, but I didn't want to expend the energy to retrieve them. I left everything there and took a cab from Baba's house to Calcutta airport. On the way, I had to stop the cab so I could relieve myself by the side of the road. The dysentery was by now raging through my body.

When I reached the airport, it was about 3:00 p.m. I was told there would be no flight to Delhi until tomorrow morning. Fortunately, there was room on a flight that I was able to book myself on.

Now what to do until 6:00 a.m? Calcutta airport was definitely a third world airport in those days, with minimum amenities. The thought of sitting in one of those plastic chairs all night made me shudder.

Fortunately, I was higher than a kite from Baba putting me in an altered state and everything had a rosy glow around it. I was not afraid. I found everything *interesting*. I moved slowly, able to focus on anything I wanted and felt warm and protected. This was my father's world and it was beautiful.

I asked a porter where I might stay for the night and he told me that there was a dormitory in the airport. I could get a cot for twenty rupees. This seemed like a great blessing to Me. I found the dormitory, which was a large room with a high ceiling and tiny windows at the top. There were perhaps twelve metal cots lined up in rows against the side walls. There were also two beds against the far wall. The men's room was back there. I took the cot on the back wall closest to it. I lay on my bed unable to sleep and watched the daylight hours pass away through the small windows at the top.

It seemed like the first time I could relax since coming to India. By now, however, I was going to the toilet every twenty minutes. Fortunately, the dormitory toilet was a western toilet, so it made things easier for me. Nonetheless things were starting to get bad. As soon as I would use the toilet, I would feel the pressure immediately begin to build again in my intestines. In a short time, I would be running back to the toilet for the next explosion. I would hurriedly sit down and a flood of water would blast out of me. It was uncontrollable. I had already trashed several pieces of underwear and other articles of clothing that I had discarded. The challenge now was to make it all the way back to New York with only the clothes I was now wearing.

By around ten o'clock at night I was exhausted. I had gotten out of bed for the umpteenth time and I was unable to sleep. I figured that I wasn't going to make it through the night if this was to continue. There was a teenage boy who was sleeping on a cot near the front door. I assumed that he was responsible for the dormitory because he took the money from people as they came in. I walked up to him, shook him awake and told him that I needed a doctor. He looked at me blankly in the dim light of a small bulb near the door. I repeated again, "I need to see a doctor. A doctor. I am sick. Can you get me a doctor?" I held out a twenty rupee note.

He now seemed to understand. He took the note, slipped his feet into his flip-flops and left the room. It was dark in the room now and people were sleeping. I thought that it might take a while for the boy to return so I decided to go back to my cot. I laid down on the cot and kept my eye on the door which I could barely make out in the darkness.

Fifteen minutes went by, then twenty, then a half hour. I had to use the toilet again. Soon after I returned to my cot the boy came in, closed the door quietly behind him, kicked off his slippers and laid down on the cot.

What the . . . .?!

Is the doctor coming? Why isn't the boy coming back to speak to me? I waited a minute or two, sat up, struggled to put my shoes on and walked back to the boy. I asked him where the doctor was, but he had his back to me and did not answer. I reached out and shook him. He turned over quickly and stared at me.

"I need a doctor," I whispered. "Where is the doctor?"

He looked at me blankly again.

Then a man who was lying on a cot behind me asked in English if I needed a doctor. I told him that I did. He told this to the boy in Bengali, repeating it several times. The boy nodded dully, sat up again, slipped on his flip-flops, got up and beckoned me to follow him.

I can still see that boy to this day. His black hair, white sleeveless tee shirt, and drab lungi. I can still hear his flip flops padding down that long gray corridor that stretched on and on, for what seemed like a mile or more. We were walking down a utility corridor with doors off of it that opened to boiler rooms, janitor closets, and mechanical rooms.

As we moved in silence on that interminable walk I began to wonder if the boy knew where he was taking me. A doctor back amid the boiler rooms?

After about five more minutes we came to a door. There was a small window beside it. The boy knocked on the door and then put his head to the glass, but it was too dark to see inside. There were no signs to indicate a doctor's office and I was not hopeful that anything would come of this. I noted the calmness of my mind and realized that under ordinary conditions I would be going ballistic by now.

The boy pounded on the door again, but nothing happened. I was now thinking that even if this was a doctor's office, he would probably have gone home for the day.

The boy pounded louder, on the window this time. I was becoming short tempered because I had to go to the toilet badly now and I didn't know how I was going to make it back to the dormitory. Baba, thy will be done.

"Come on," I said, "let's go back."

The boy eyed me hesitantly. I started walking and the boy reluctantly began to follow me. Suddenly a light went on and the door opened. An old man stuck his gray, balding head out the door and squinted at us. He was tall and thin and wore a dhoti and a long-sleeved crumpled white shirt. The boy told him our situation and the man invited us in.

We entered a tiny room with a crudely poured concrete floor and dull white walls. In the middle of the room was an examination table and along the wall a shelf and a small cabinet. The old man motioned for me to get on the table.

I told him hurriedly that I had to use the toilet. He motioned to a curtain. I pushed it back and found the typical set up. After relieving myself, I went back into the room and sat on the table. I remember thinking that this doctor must have slept on his examination table. Did he live here? In my present state I couldn't tell if this was strange or it was just me.

Fortunately, the doctor spoke enough English so that I could communicate my symptoms to him. He was missing a front tooth and smiled continually. He took my temperature and gave me a half dozen large white pills. Two pills now. Two pills in the morning. Two the next evening. He said I would be okay. Hmmm.

I gave the "doctor" twenty rupees (about two dollars) and the boy and I left. When we reached the dormitory, I went to the toilet again. I felt a little insecure because I had hoped the pills would have begun to kick in a little. I wanted to sleep, but was wide awake. As I lay there, I could feel the pressure in my gut building again. The pills did not seem to be working. After five minutes I was up again heading for the toilet. I was exhausted now and it was difficult to move. When I got up from the toilet this time and turned to flush it, the water was bright red. "Not good," I thought.

I struggled back to my bed and fell face down on it. I found myself unable to move—too weak to pull myself further up on the cot or to turn over. I thought of my family, of Ellen and Flora waiting for me in New York. I thought of my business partners. I felt mysteriously calm and content. My heart still surged with bliss. I realized that everything was in God's hands. I found myself thinking of the movie "Little Big Man" where the Indian chief in the midst of having his entire village wiped out by marauding soldiers, smiles serenely and says "It's a good day to die." I was shocked when he said it. But now I understood it.

I did not have long to nurture such thoughts, however, because almost immediately I heard Baba's voice in my head ordering me to "Sit up."

"Sit up." He said again in a no-nonsense tone of voice.

I became amused at this phenomenon and lay there contemplating it when again Baba told me to "Sit up," but now the voice was angry and commanding. It jolted me to my senses. I struggled to turn over and with much determination I succeeded in doing so. I managed to prop myself against the wall.

Then Baba said firmly, "Now do your spiritual practices."

Despite Baba's words, I was losing consciousness. It wasn't like going to sleep. I thought I was probably dying.

Again, I heard the Guru's voice. "Do your spiritual practices." He was again very angry with me, perhaps for allowing myself to slip away. I struggled to focus my mind. I didn't want to come back. I inhaled deeply and began to say my mantra. The sound of the mantra in my mind was the last thing I remember.

When I opened my eyes the dim light of morning was coming through the little windows. I'm alive, I thought. It did not seem especially remarkable now. In fact, everything seemed almost normal. With some effort, I slid to the edge of the cot and put my shoes on. I then got up and found my way to the terminal. Fifteen people or so were standing in a queue for the flight to Delhi. I walked to the head of the line and told people that I was ill. I asked them if I could "cut in line." They immediately moved back from me, eyeing me in silence as if I carried the Black Plague.

I was the first to board the airplane. I did not take a seat on the plane. I walked to one of the toilets and locked myself in. No one bothered me. It was an experience blasting off while sitting on the toilet.

Once the seatbelt lights were off, people began to rattle the handle and knock on the door. I didn't say anything. I didn't budge. I could tell that a couple of people were really angry, but there wasn't anything I could do about it. I was monopolizing half of the toilet facilities on the plane. Luckily one was not for men, the other for women. I don't know what would have happened then. As it was, I sat tight for two hours.

Landing on a flying toilet I found was rougher than taking off on one. During the descent the big plane creaked and dipped and made me feel sea sick. I got quite a jolt when the wheels touched down and was slammed into the metal sink when the pilot hit the brakes and put up the flaps.

I waited for the plane to stop before I pulled up my pants and then waited a little longer for the commotion outside the door to die down. When I finally stuck my head out, I could see the last few people getting off the plane. I joined the back of the line, said goodbye to the smiling stewardesses and walked into the Delhi airport.

New Delhi

It was midmorning when we arrived at the Delhi airport. I found the Air India counter and inquired as to the next flight to New York. The man told me that the three o'clock flight was cancelled because of smog.

"Smog?"

"Yes sir, I'm sorry."

"You're joking, right?"

"No sir.

I stood there trying to get my bearings.

"When will the next flight be leaving?"

"I'm not sure, the flight scheduled for tomorrow may be cancelled also."

"What?" I gawked.

"Sir," he said wearily, "I'm telling what the computer says. It may change. We don't know at this point."

I regained my composure, realizing that the clerk was as much a victim of circumstances as I was.

"Please book me for the next available flight."

I waited while the man reviewed my return ticket, passport, and checked the computer. Everything was in order. I was now scheduled to be on the next flight. Whenever that might be.

"Can you recommend a hotel near the airport where I can rest until flight time?"

"I'm sorry, sir, all the hotels around the airport are booked due to flight cancellations."

"Do you know that for a fact?" I asked sincerely.

"Yes, sir."

The man looked honest enough to turn his mother in for a minor traffic violation. I thanked him and left the counter. I found a seating area near a men's room and sat down.

Now what should I do? I didn't feel like reading anything. I didn't want to look at souvenirs. I didn't have an appetite. Basically, I had nothing to keep me occupied with the prospect of sitting there for hours, perhaps days.

I closed my eyes to meditate. In my heightened state of consciousness, I quickly lost all contact with my physical reality. When I came to, I felt that I was going to go in my pants again. I hurried into the men's room. In the Delhi airport the toilets were the holes in the floor type. As I struggled to get my shoes off so I could take my pants off, I couldn't hold back. My socks, lungota and pants all got sprayed. Lord God!

There were two things that consoled me about this nightmare. The first was that miraculously there was no longer any blood in my stool. The second was that as bad as this mess looked, it didn't smell bad. For the first time in my life I could say that my sh*t didn't stink. Sorry, I couldn't resist.

For the present, however, I was in a quandary because I had no other clothes to wear. When I no longer heard anybody outside my stall, I walked out and threw my socks and lungota into the trash. Then butt-naked I walked over to one of the sinks and began to wash my pants in the basin using the hand soap. I kept hoping nobody would come in, but of course things got very busy all of a sudden. As guys came in, I could see that jolt of recognition slit across their faces. It said there was a major nutcase loose in the men's room. But then they would go about their business as if nothing unusual was happening. Being able to suspend disbelief is a great survival mechanism. I don't get uptight. They don't get uptight. Things work out fine.

The process seriously bogged me down, however, when I had to stand in front of the hand dryer waving my pants back and forth under it to dry them. This was very time consuming and having to continually punch the knob to restart the blower was exhausting me.

At some point an Indian boy about sixteen years old came into the room. He looked like he might have been working in the airport. I offered him twenty rupees to take over the drying operation and he agreed. It was all done with sign language, but no problem.

I sat on the floor where the floor was semi-dry and clean and watched the boy. I was holding my wallet and passport in my lap. Now the look on the faces of the men who entered was no longer one of fear, but of puzzlement.

In time the job was done and I paid the boy. My pants were now clean and warm and I felt particularly civilized again. I returned to my chair in the seating area and watched the people come and go for an hour or so until I began to feel tired and weak again. I was having trouble sitting up straight.

A European man, who had come to the seating area, was now sitting across from me and kept looking at me. He asked me if I needed help. I thanked him, but told him I didn't think there was anything that he could do. Talking to him, however, reminded me of the pills in my shirt pocket that the "doctor" in the Calcutta airport had given me last night. I excused myself and went to find a bottle of water. When I found a bottle at a concession stand, I took the pills.

I returned to my seat and the man was still there. He asked if I had eaten recently. I told him no.

"Would you like some food?"

"No, thank you. I'm okay."

"Is there nothing I can get you?"

"No, thank you." I was tired and I didn't feel like talking.

"Would you like a sandwich?" He began opening a back pack beside him.

"Thank you, sir, but I'm not hungry."

"How about a banana. Perhaps you should at least eat a banana. I have some bananas here."

He fumbled in his back pack and pulled out a small bunch of bananas. Actually, they looked good to me. I told him I would have one.

After he gave me the banana, he seemed to feel better. He wished me luck and walked away. I sat there eating the banana. It was the first solid food I had in a week. Bananas are such a light food, but today I felt like I was eating a chunk of clay.

It was a very strange sensation because I could actually feel the banana as it slid down my throat, gurgle through my stomach, then ooze through my intestines and come out the other end. It was unbelievable. The process took about twenty minutes and I was back in the men's room.

I now slid into a funk. I felt alone and insecure. Everything was too strange. I took a little walk and became so exhausted that I had to sit down on the floor because no seating area was close by. I watched the people bustling on their way. Everyone looked intent. A ragtag beggar walked by me and I thought how fortunate he was to have the power of mobility, to know where he was going. I realized that no one noticed me.

I was caught in a vast tiled-floor purgatory somewhere between heaven and home—a surreal place of loneliness where nothing changed. What's worse is that I knew that if people would speak to me, they would have nothing to say. Nor I in return.

In the next instance my altered state reasserted itself and I burst out laughing at the cosmic joke of it all and could not stop. I had been in the tent of God, laid on His pillows, and drank His wine. He held my hand and squeezed my cheeks and sent me out into the world with a big bear hug that changed me into a happy, glowing ball of light. I was way up there. The Guru was in life and death and so was I. The Guru was higher than the highest and lower than the lowest and so was I. As I laid there close to death in the Delhi airport I found myself soaring like an angel.

After some time, reality again straightened its tie and knocked on my door. I got myself up and found my way back to the Air India counter. I told the man that I was deathly ill and that I might die in the airport if I had to stay here too much longer. I told him that he must find a way out for me. He looked at me earnestly and realized that I was not joking. His fingers began to fly over the keyboard and his eyes peered intently at his computer screen. Nothing. Nothing. Wait.

"I have something. There is a small airline flight going to Bombay at 4:00 p.m. this afternoon and from Bombay, there is a flight to New York tomorrow morning at 5:00 a.m. Do you want to do that?"

I could have kissed him. He checked further and discovered available seating on both flights.

The flight to Bombay was another one spent locked in the toilet. More frustration from the passengers. The stewardess even knocked once and I told her I was sick. She didn't say anything more, the knocking stopped and the rest of the flight went off without a hitch. I'm sure the whole plane knew I was in there though.

Blown Away in Bombay

When I landed in Bombay (Mumbai) a policeman spotted me as soon as I had deplaned and walked into the terminal. He immediately became very excited and started calling to people down a hallway that I couldn't see. He looked almost comical in his state of agitation, like a Keystone Cop in a Mack Sennett movie. A strange sensation came over me that he was Baba. In fact, by now I suspected that Baba had shaped himself into every atom of my environment.

The policeman came running to me dragging his leg and yelling over his shoulder. He grabbed me by the waist and held me up. Soon two men and a wheelchair came careening around a corner. The police officer and the men lowered me into the wheel chair and off we went double-time down the hallway.

At the end of the hallway I was wheeled into a room that looked like an official clinic. A team of three people in white coats helped me onto a table and questioned me about my illness. I told them the whole story. "You have dysentery," they said and gave me more pills. They were a cheery lot.

Without me requesting anything from them, they booked me into a hotel and ordered an ambulance to take me there. Suddenly I was being treated like royalty. Where was all of this headed?

At the hotel I was wheeled into the most sumptuous lobby I had ever seen. The room was cast in yellow marble with long, sparkling chandeliers and hanging gardens. A large fountain in the center of the room splashed softly while guests lounged around it having drinks from marble tables covered in white linen.

At the check-in counter I was assigned a room and was told that the ambulance would return at 4:00 a.m. to take me to the airport. The hotel clerk informed me that they would give me a wakeup call at 3:15 a.m., if that was acceptable. I looked at him and realized that I had fallen into the Alice in Wonderland hole and my eyes searched the room for the Cheshire Cat's grin.

A porter put me on the elevator and wheeled me to my room. We entered a richly decorated room with plush furniture, a queen-sized bed, and wall to wall carpeting. I got out of the wheelchair, tipped the porter and closed the door.

I was alone. It felt good. I even had a little energy. I sat down on a plush chair by the bed and the telephone rang.

"Yes, this is Mr. Paprocki. "Some yogurt and tea? Sure, that would be fine."

In five minutes, another porter was at the door carrying a silver tray. He came into the room and placed the tray on the table beside the bed. He left before I could tip him. I only had a fifty rupee note so I was glad.

The yogurt for some reason was incredibly delicious. The tea warmed my insides. I felt Baba huddled around me like an old grandmother. The feeling was palpable and it filled me up. I savored the yogurt and took a few more sips of tea. Not counting the banana at the Delhi airport, this was the first food I had eaten in a week. It seemed as if I was experiencing the sense of taste for the first time in my life.

When I finished, I pulled my toothbrush out of my pants pocket and walked into the bathroom. There were two lush white bath towels sitting on a chair, an ornate medicine cabinet above a sink with gold faucets and a gleaming, long, white bathtub. As I stood there gawking at the bathtub, the thought of a hot bath brought tears to my eyes. I hadn't had access to hot water since I came to India. I was able to stretch out my entire body. And when I turned the tap off, the room became absolutely still. I felt the heat soften my tight muscles, I felt the water on my chin and listened to the ringing in my ears. I sunk deeper into consciousness.

From the time that Baba had spoken inside my mind at the Calcutta airport dormitory until this very moment, I had felt him pulsing inside me. I could feel him as a presence. If I needed something, I only had to think of it and I would be taken care of. I felt a nucleus to my being that protected me from the waves of outside events. Now, as I lay in the water, this spirit began to pulsate out of my being and permeate the water. The water began to brim with spirit. It continued to spread into the bathtub. The bathtub shimmered. The room began to fill with a soft glow. I was immersed in a palpable light and could no longer tell where "I" began or where "I" ended. God was inside me and outside me. I was inside me and outside me. Relative reality had melted down and I had entered a reality that was much more fluid. "This or that" was now "this is that." I laid there in the bliss until the water got cold. But even as I got out of the tub, and walked around, I felt that my self was filling up the room. It was a very strange yet somehow familiar feeling.

One more interesting thing happened before I fell to sleep that night. It was after 9:00 p.m. by the time that I got out of the bathtub. I looked at my pile of rumpled clothes on the floor and had a desire for fresh clean clothes. Wouldn't it be nice to meet Ellen and Flora wearing fresh clothes, I thought.

I called the front desk and asked the man if he knew a store nearby where I might buy some western style clothes. The man said that it was Saturday night and that it was unlikely that I would find a store open tonight. He, nonetheless, asked my shirt and pants sizes and said he would see what he could find out. I knew that he would find a place for me, but when I heard a knock on my door a half hour later and a porter walked in with the new clothes, I was still amazed. The porter asked if I would like him to take my soiled clothes to be laundered. They would be ready by 4:00 a.m. in time for my departure. "Really?" I said. He took my dirty clothes with him.

The next morning, I forgot about getting my clothes back from the hotel and left without them. My new clothes fit a little tight but they would do. The odd thing was, in looking back, I never paid for the clothes. I never paid for the hotel either. They had taken my credit card number when I entered the hotel, but I was never billed for my room or my new clothes. The night was on the house. Oddly, I never learned what hotel I had stayed in. Some hotel in Bombay. There wasn't a need to know any more than that.

The ambulance arrived on time and I got on the plane without incident. Next stop London, and then on to New York City. I decided to take my seat on the plane rather than monopolize the toilet. For some mysterious reason, the constant nagging in my gut had vanished. Maybe I was cured!? I was still very weak and my skin still felt like wood, but I began to think that in light of the past evenings miraculous happenings, I might be getting better.

Once we were off the ground, however, my hopes were dashed. The pressure in my gut began to build again with deadly force. I had to move quickly down the aisle to the toilet. Luckily, the room was vacant and I made it okay. But as I sat there in that little red cubicle I thought about what lied ahead for me. Twelve hours of flight time on a toilet? The thought withered my sense of self-confidence. I couldn't do it. But then again, I had to do it. If I was unable to get to the toilet just one time, I'd have diarrhea all over me, with no change of clothes.

I began to talk to Baba. I said "Baba, listen to me. I am your son. You love me. Please help me to keep my sense of human dignity. What can I do? I am in your hands, Baba."

There was a contradiction in this plea that my mind immediately began to wrestle with. If I was asking for help, this implied that God did not know the best thing for me and needed me to remind him. I should just surrender to God's will and take whatever came, because this would be the best thing to do in the face of multiple consequences that I could never know or understand.

But suddenly, there was Baba's sweet, soothing voice again inside my mind. "Don't be alarmed, my boy. You have nothing to fear. Everything will be okay." Then, something happened that I don't know how to describe. I guess you could say I had a vision. I saw a tiger stalking through thick underbrush in a jungle. In my fluid state of mind, the tiger was real to me and I felt frightened. At first the tiger didn't notice me, but as the pressure in my intestines began to build again, he became more restless. As the pressure built, the tiger's movements became more disturbed as if he sensed a kill. I knew he was now seeking me out and I became terrified. I now realized that the tiger was the dysentery and I was his prey. The tiger now was close at hand. He saw me and quickened his pace to attack. I knew that any second he would leap and the explosion would tear my guts out again. "Watch him now, my son, watch him! Don't take your eyes off him. Watch him. The instant before he leaps you must attack." The tiger slowed his pace slightly when he saw my resolve, but kept coming. My body tightened like coiled steel. I watched the tiger's eyes intently as he came at me. And then I saw it in his eyes—the message that told him to leap. But before he did, I leaped at the tiger with all the adrenaline in my body, yelling my mantra like a war cry inside my brain. The tiger flinched, fell away to the side, and trotted off into the brush.

I had done it! I had gained control over the explosive convulsions that had wracked my body for the last eight days. This was an extraordinary accomplishment and something that I would never have thought of in a million years.

"How are you doing now, my child," I heard Baba say.

"I am fine Baba," I said. "By your grace I am fine."

I returned to my seat with my human dignity intact. From that moment I knew how to face the tiger of fear. This knowledge has come in handy many times in my life. There is nothing that God will not do for his children if they all willing to know Him.

London

The plane made a stop at Heathrow airport in London for an hour to refuel. Everyone got out and stretched their legs. I remained on the plane and watched a small crew of women in blue coveralls board the plane. They made their way down the aisle to me with vacuum cleaners and large plastic garbage cans. Speaking in a heavy Cockney accent, they talked about a lazy boyfriend of one of their friends, completely ignoring me. No one even glanced at me. It seemed a natural part of the exotic dream through which I was now living. In a short time, the cleaning ladies disappeared, the plane filled up again and we were off the ground.

New York

After six hours we landed in Kennedy airport. It was now 12:30 a.m. on Monday morning New York time. I was dazed and crabby and felt weak and vulnerable. When I exited the plane, I asked for a wheelchair and someone came with one in a few minutes. I didn't have to wait for luggage, but I did have to wait in line for customs. After passing through customs, the attendant wheeled me to the exit doors of the terminal where I was hoping to get a cab. As he pushed me through the sliding glass doors a heavy sheet of cold rain whipped around us and chilled me instantly to the bone. I moaned in despair and the attendant pulled me back inside the doors.

Now what? I sat facing the closed, rain streaked doors unable to see a thing in the blackness beyond. I sat freezing now in the air-conditioning.

The attendant asked him if he could flag a cab for me. The cop walked over and glared down at me.

"What the hell's the matter with you?"

"Dysentery."

"Dysentery," he sneered loudly. "Jesus Christ."

He was shaking his head at me as if I was the biggest ***hole he ever met. Then he turned and walked out into the rain.

In about five minutes he came back in and grabbed the handles of the wheelchair from the attendant. He pushed me through the glass doors and out into the blasting cold rain.

"Ooh," I moaned.

"Yeah, yeah, yeah" he grumbled derisively.

He wheeled me through the rain to a cab waiting on the curb. He opened the back door, picked me up and sat me on the seat. Then he pushed my legs into the cab and slammed the door. "Thank you, officer," I said weakly, but he didn't hear me.

I told the cab driver my address and asked him to turn up the heat. He was an old black guy who made me feel safe. I laid down on the seat and listened to the driving rain and the click of the windshield wipers for some time before I fell asleep. I did not wake until we stopped on the street outside my apartment building.

I asked the driver if he would call Ellen from the phone on the corner. He looked back at me as if to say I had a lot of nerve. I knew it was a lot to ask from a NY cabbie, but I didn't think I could make it up the four flights of stairs by myself. The old man made the call for me and came back and opened the car door for me. It was now about 2:00 a.m.

"She says she'll be right down," he said. I felt good. I was home! My beautiful Ellen, my sweet little Flora. I was finally home. I had made it by God's grace.

The old man walked me to the front door of my building. As we arrived at the stoop, the door opened. There stood Ellen and Flora. An odd mix of happiness and fear swept their face as they looked at me. I paid the old man and I walked up the stairs with Flora on one side and Ellen on the other.

The next morning when Ellen took Flora to school, I put on my suit and went to the office. I would not have Jan and Shaam believe I was not a man of my word. It was a matter of principle that I show up for work as I promised, especially in light of our bad parting.

Fortunately, when they saw me, they became immediately alarmed and began making phone calls to friends and acquaintances asking for leads to a specialist in internal medicine. They found one, a Dr. Greene, who was an internist at NYU Hospital. Jan scheduled an appointment for Tuesday afternoon and Shaam told me to go home. I was obviously no use to anybody in my condition. Jan and Shaam were helpful but stiff. I could still feel the anger and resentment simmering below the surface.

I walked the fifteen blocks from the office to my apartment through the blasting rush and clatter of the city. By the time I reached my apartment I was exhausted again. The headiness of my state of mind was still holding true, but my body was shriveling up and dying.

I knew I had to get to a hospital immediately. Ellen was all too willing to get me to the emergency room, angered as she was by my going to work.

We took a cab to New York University Hospital on 1st Avenue and 32nd Street and went through triage. I quickly discovered that while I might be dying, it wasn't an emergency. I would have to wait with everyone else until a doctor could see me. Ellen and I sat down along the wall and waited. We waited for over an hour and by now Ellen was pissed. She normally had a short fuse, but this was kicking her over the top. She kept going up to the receptionist's window and demanding attention for me. I was finding it difficult to sit up straight, but I was still in good spirits. I was trying to calm Ellen but to no avail. After having gone through the events of the last week, I knew I was going to be fine, but she didn't. She thought I was going to die any second and my guru and this hospital be damned.

Now Ellen was yelling at the receptionist about the incompetence of the hospital and threatening to sue them for negligence. After a couple of minutes of this harangue, which gained the attention of the entire waiting room, an orderly barged through a couple of swinging doors with a metal table on wheels and helped me on to it. He wheeled me down the hall and parked me behind a curtain beside an empty table. He left me there. I couldn't tell if this was progress or I was being punished.

I stayed there about ten minutes in the dark quiet and then I felt the pressure begin to build again in me. At the same time, the orderly returned and pulled me back down the hall into a large room filled with doctors, nurses and tables. The orderly parked me sideways inside a small cubicle defined by sliding curtains. He slapped a paper hospital gown on the foot of the table then left.

I struggled to sit up, undress and put the gown on. The pressure inside me was becoming painful and I couldn't concentrate to stop it. I tried to see the tiger in my mind, but it was too scattered. The pain got worse. I began waving to people and telling them I needed help, but it was too late. I heard the stuff splatter all over the floor. That got people's attention. A couple of orderlies immediately came over. They washed me up and helped me back on to the table. Another guy came over with a mop and bucket to clean the floor. He was wearing rubber boots and rubber gloves. As I lay there watching him, I began to consider that I might not have dysentery. What if I was a carrier of a rare, contagious virus or bacteria? What if I was a dead man after all? What if everyone I breathed on or touched was to?

As I pondered these sobering thoughts, a beautiful woman doctor walked up to me and asked me how I was feeling. I smiled at her. Fine, I said. She smiled back.

"So what's the story?"

"I just returned from India yesterday," I said. "I think I have dysentery."

"Let's hope so," she replied.

She took my temperature and drew some blood. She had trouble locating a vein because of the hardness of my skin. She gave me a sidelong glance. My somber thoughts vanished with her attention.

"I'm going to irrigate you and then I've got to send you home."

Irrigate me? Send me home? I told her about my appointment with Dr. Greene tomorrow.

"Oh, so now you're doing my job for me," she quipped.

The doctor called over a nurse and instructed him. He strapped a bag of glucose to a pole and pulled it up beside my head. Then he slipped a needle on the syringe and flicked it until the glucose ran through it. He ran his hands up and down my arm and even turned my hand over looking for a vein. He shook his head. He stuck me a couple of times but couldn't find anything. Finally, he found a vein and taped the needle down.

After making sure everything was okay, he left. I laid there for a couple of hours alternately meditating and watching the clear liquid drip slowly drop by drop down the syringe. When the bag was empty, a nurse came and unhooked me and sent me home. Ellen had been waiting for me and walked me outside. She waved down a cab and we went home. She told me that the doctor who had seen me had asked her if I was gay. She thought I might have AIDS.

The next day, I saw Dr. Greene. He had the results of my blood test from the day before. He told me that I had a rare form of bacterial dysentery. There were no pills that I could take to kill it. There was, fortunately, an antibiotic in a serum form that they could give me. This was fine with the doctor because it could be administered to me in the glucose that I would need every day to rehydrate me.

The bad news was there were no rooms available in the hospital because of the AIDS epidemic. It was an epidemic that was not in the newspapers, but it was serious enough so that AIDS victims were growing faster than there were hospital rooms to accommodate them. Room turnover in the hospitals was becoming a rare phenomenon.

Dr. Greene told me that the NYU hospital retained two floors of rooms that were not served by nurses. I could get into one of these rooms if I had someone to sign me in and take care of me day and night. I couldn't imagine who that could be. I left the office on the hope that a room would open soon.

The next day after Ellen took Flora to school and went to work, I had the apartment to myself. My head was foggy and my body was exhausted. I laid in bed in a bizarre sort of stupor. Ellen had put a bucket by the bedside for emergencies. It was late morning when I fell into a deep sleep. It was a different kind of sleep and I was aware of its strange quality even as I slept.

It was a sleep that took me deeper and deeper below wakeful consciousness. It was like sinking below the ocean. I went down to a realm of consciousness that I had never been to before. It was as if I was entering the internal workings of the universe itself. Great sprocketed wheels, perhaps a hundred stories high, and giant black slabs the size of football fields churned ponderously by, sliding in and out of each other as well as other great archetypal forms in a slow complex, syncopated movement. I watched the process, mesmerized for a long time. I could no longer tell up from down, in from out, wakefulness from sleep. I didn't know what I was looking at or where I was. I had no sense of past or future. When I struggled to remember something, I couldn't remember anything. Remembering meant nothing. But there was something. A small sense of alarm had begun to enter me. I began to feel that something was seriously wrong. But what was it? What was the matter? I couldn't put my finger on it. And then it suddenly hit me. I wasn't alive anymore. I was dead.

Simultaneous with the shock of this recognition, I found myself in a room of stone. In the center of the room was a large round pool of water enclosed by a two-foot high wall. Steam rose from the water and on the wall sat a large washer woman. Her long skirt was pulled above her knees and her white, coarse blouse was soaked with sweat. She held a big ball of clothing in her hands and was beating it fiercely against the top of the wall.

When she caught sight of me out of the corner of her eye, she whirled quickly to face me. Her mouth opened into a wide maniacal gap-toothed grin. "Welcome," she cackled.

The laughter that followed reverberated in the stony room and filled my guts with an inky dread. Fear skittered up my spine and sucked my lungs inside out. I was in a life and death struggle to breathe. The turmoil of fear and the heaving and gasping for breath brought me back to wakeful consciousness. "Who I am," came churning up slowly from the depths and broke the placid surface of day to day reality. But even as I woke, and bolted upright in bed, I still did not know who or where I was. What I looked at, I didn't recognize. What I saw had no name. After several minutes my breathing became more stable. It dawned on me slowly that I was looking out my bedroom window through a shelf filled with plants. The sun was shining bright outside. I could hear cars on the street and chatter from people in the outdoor café across the street.

Later in the afternoon, I looked in the Yellow Pages under Nurses. I was hoping to hire a nurse to watch me in the special hospital wing. The cost of a full-time nurse was six hundred dollars per day. I called my insurance company. They would not cover the cost. I had to drop the idea because I'd blow through my savings in a matter of a few days.

Ellen and Flora came home after an hour or so and we had dinner. The food felt strange in my mouth and I didn't eat much. Ellen and Flora watched me furtively. I tried to keep an upbeat face so they wouldn't be frightened, but I wasn't myself and they were definitely frightened. In truth, having the illness in my own home made my appearance and behavior stand out in stark contrast to my normal state of being. When I sat down on the couch after dinner to help Flora with her homework, I didn't have the strength to do it. She was afraid to touch me because of the way my skin felt. Flora told me years later that she was very angry and upset with Baba for doing this to me. I never was able to explain to her what actually was going on.

Ellen came into the room and began to help Flora with her work. I began looking through my address book for someone who could sign me into the hospital and stay with me for a few days. Only one name in the entire book was an option, but even he was a remote possibility. It was Ben Olsen. Ben's father owned one of the biggest parking garage operations in Manhattan. He owned and managed garages all over the city.

When I first came to New York, I parked cars in a garage that Ben's father bought and thereafter I became his employee. In this way, I met Ben whose job it was to make the round of garages and check up on the managers. Ben was my age and when he came by my garage on east 26th Street, we'd drink coffee and shoot the breeze. We talked about writing and art and philosophy. We even got together a few times off the job and went for a beer or to a restaurant. All this happened before I met Ellen and while Flora was living with me after her mother had moved to Chicago. Ben was self-absorbed and he'd easily become resentful and even angry with Flora for demanding my attention when we were together. Flora was only about six years old then. I had to stop socializing with Ben for this reason. As I looked at his name in my address book, I realized that it was a couple of years since I had seen him. It made me uneasy to call him now and ask such a big favor especially after having brushed him off. I was desperate though and I knew that Ben would have no trouble taking off from work if he agreed to help me.

I called Ben and, surprisingly, he agreed to help me out. In an hour or so he showed up and after brief introductions, he took me to the hospital to be registered. Ben had to fill out forms saying that he would be responsible for me. After the formalities, the receptionist told us where the room was located and it turned out to be pretty nice. It had two single beds in it and the floor was carpeted.

After a couple of hours of me dozing in and out and being bad company and Ben running in and out of the room to have a cigarette, he got bored and decided to leave. He said he'd be back to check on me in the morning. I became upset, thinking they might throw me out. But thank God no one from the hospital came to check on me that night.

The next morning, Ben came back about 10:00 a.m. and, according to instructions, wheeled me down to a room where they took more blood and hooked me up to another bag of glucose. This one had the serum in it. It took two hours to empty into my arm and then Ben wheeled me back upstairs. He was hyper from having to wait around for two hours. He said that he had to leave and he walked out again.

I fell asleep. When I awoke, I found a tray of food beside my bed. I ate it because there was nothing else to do. Ben called in the evening to say he couldn't make it back to the hospital. I told him it was okay. Whatever.

The next day, I walked down to get my glucose by myself. Nobody said anything about Ben not being with me and I breathed a sigh of relief.

Later in the afternoon, Shaam came by. He was still stiff and businesslike. He was full of information about my health insurance coverage and assured me that my hospital bills would be paid. He told me that Jan and he were covering for me and that I should do what I needed to do to get well. His words were cool, but he was doing the right thing. I asked him about the Intelsat job we were working on when I left. Surprisingly, only a week had passed since I had left New York and returned, but it seemed like a lifetime. Shaam told me that no action had been taken. We were exactly where we were on the day that I left.

Later, we learned that one of the administrators at Intelsat was caught defrauding the organization and was fired. Intelsat then decided it was best to keep a low profile and dropped our ad campaign all together. How ironic. Our big chance had come and gone and my visit to see Baba had no impact on that process whatsoever. At the time it appeared like seeing Baba would jeopardize the chance of a lifetime.

The next couple of days passed uneventfully. I went downstairs each morning. They took my blood and gave me glucose. My skin began to feel a little more like flesh now and I was beginning to feel a little more human. In the afternoons and evenings I would meditate, read, and sleep. An orderly would bring me meals and take the empty trays. Other than this, I saw no one.

It would take another twenty-five days before I was well enough to leave the hospital. I came out just before Christmas and I was home for the holidays.

The spirit of Christmas shimmered in the air. I knew that I would never be the same. I had seen God face to face and had lived through it. I didn't know what it meant, but I knew the journey was not over. I felt, however, that I had gotten another clue. And somehow, I would have to make it work in New York with a wife and daughter and an advertising agency on 5th Avenue. Of this much I was sure. God was alive and well and able to live in a human body. I knew that it might take a while, but that when God does this sort of thing, it usually means big changes for humanity. For me personally there was even a greater revelation that Baba had provided me. His body didn't matter. God was a conscious force whose expression moved in and out of forms at will. He had been inside my mind, outside in the things that surrounded me, in my life, in my death, in a body, out of a body, in my pain, and in my bliss. God was everywhere at once. These things philosophers and saints have talked about, but by God's grace, I had personally experienced them.

I knew from what Baba had told us that if I continued to meditate on Oneness, the difference between "inside me" and "outside me" would eventually break down completely. Every contradiction in my thoughts would eventually melt into God consciousness as surely as waves hit the shore and melt back into the sea. My self and God Self would become one.

I also realized that it didn't matter if anyone believed me or not. It didn't matter if anyone realized who Baba was or not. It didn't matter if everyone believed their guru was God, or if they didn't believe in gurus at all. It didn't matter if they believed Jesus is God, or Buddha, or Mohammed (upon him be peace), Krishna, or Shiva. Or if they believe that God is impersonal like the Om sound or the white light. As for me, I realized that God is the stuff of which all forms are made. God is Consciousness itself—a loving consciousness. If you have Absolute Consciousness you are God. If you think you are an individual consciousness you are not God. If you are

Absolute Consciousness you exist in all forms. The universe is your mind. In this universe you play hide and seek with your children. It is your fun. And your children, if they want you, they will have to find you. To do this, everything they hold dear will have to be given away. They will have to spend themselves down.

Part Four

A Matter Of Style

I made a good amount of money for the business my first year back from India and my partners eventually calmed down. It was a prosperous time for us. We didn't get rich, but we made enough money to live the lifestyle that we wanted. We could pay for health insurance, dental bills, enjoy a gym membership, and take vacations. We could even save a little.

My visit to see Baba had inspired me to work for his mission again. I got Proutist Universal, the organization that promoted Prout, recognized as an affiliate organization with the United Nations. This allowed us to attend UN briefings and international conferences, use the UN library, and more importantly, work with other nonprofit organizations to further our mutual agendas.

I wrote a couple of booklets at this time, "Prout and Economic Decentralization" and "Prout Politics" that we circulated at conferences. I also began to attend the briefings at UN headquarters on 1st Avenue. My partners knew now that business would never claim my whole attention and so long as we were making money, they were okay with this.

Things moved along nicely until Black Monday, October 13, 1987 when the stock market took its worst free fall since the Great Depression. From that date forward the work we received from our real estate clients slowly shrunk to a trickle. Within a year we were hurting and things were turning sour. We began to skip pay checks. Shaam began to freak out under the pressure and become an angry man. He began to scream at Jan and me and make threats about closing the business. "Sales, sales, sales," he would yell.

Shaam wanted me to become as upset as he was. He wanted me to commit my life to the business. I sympathized with his position, but I resented his abusive manner. Although a part of me was as frightened as he was, I had the benefit of knowing that I was in God's hands. I could get through a shakeup. And personally, my stomach for devoting my life to making money for large real estate companies was reaching its limit. I wasn't in the mood to redouble my efforts. Actually, I wanted to do more Prout work. Life at Commercial*ARTS*, therefore, became more strained with each passing day.

I was sitting in my office one day wondering if I should call Jones Lang Wootton for the third time in a week to see if they had considered our bid on a project when out of the blue I received a call from Greg Herschel. Greg was an Ananda Margi and a Proutist, who had been an organizer with me in Carbondale in the early days. He now lived in Washington DC and held an administrative post with the Department of Education. I liked Greg, he had grace and style and a good sense of humor.

Greg told me that he had gotten an unusual call from a mutual friend, Dean Greenberg. Dean had been the youngest monk Ananda Marga ever produced at the tender age of eighteen. Dean was banned from seeing Baba, however, after he rejected a posting during Indira Gandhi's State of Emergency. The pressure on him was too great. After barely escaping India with his life, he gave up his acharyaship. Dean was also one of the Carbondale crew. He and Greg went back to high school days.

While I had kept contact with Greg, since both of us were on the east coast, I had pretty much lost contact with Dean after I had moved to New York. He had moved to Denver Colorado about the same time that I had left Carbondale. From time to time I would hear that he had become a very successful business consultant in the automobile industry. He had remarried, owned a big house, fast car, gold watch, and was living the American Dream. But now Greg was telling me that Dean had become very unhappy with the direction that his life had taken. He was coming to Washington DC to visit with Greg. He wondered if it was possible if the two of them could pay me a visit in NYC sometime over the coming weekend.

"Sure," I said.

"Great."

When I hung up the phone, I was in a better mood than I had been for weeks. These guys were more than old friends. They were my "brothers." We saw reality through the same eyes. We knew Baba. When we talked, we were like family, no matter the distance in time or space between us.

Greg had an attorney friend, Scott Hudgeons, who worked for an international law firm that kept an apartment in the city. Scott was a Margi too, but I didn't know him. He arranged to get Greg the keys to the apartment. The place was only a few blocks from my apartment and we met at the Gemini Diner on 2nd Avenue and 35th Street at 9:00 a.m. on Saturday morning. It was a sunny day in July, 1990.

Over breakfast, Dean and I caught up on almost ten years of living since we had parted company.

We had been very close when we were together. He was one of the core leaders of our unit and we had worked side by side on many projects, including the Shawnee Prison Project. Dean and I had been in the belly of the beast together and had sorted through a lot of crap to discover how our government really worked behind the scenes.

We picked up our conversation with the same ease as if we were sitting in our office debriefing after a day's activity. I could feel the weight and nuance of each word he spoke. Through his stories, told in good humor and laced with jokes and anecdotes, I could see that Greg was right; he was in pain and confusion. He had married a woman who was obsessed with achieving the American Dream, obsessed with material possessions, obsessed with the pretense of happiness as if there were nothing else to reality. He was surrounded by friends and business associates who shared the same values as his wife and who paid him big money to increase their sales. Dean's gift was that he could read anybody and sell them anything. It was like a science. He had a gift of gab that could put you in an etheric state and have you nodding yes to anything he wanted to sell. Businesses, even the biggest companies, wanted a piece of Dean.

The problem was that he had achieved his gold card and two car garage just to see if he could do it. Dean had another dream. He was like me. He wanted God. But he had gotten side tracked and was now feeling trapped.

I told him what he wanted to hear. The spiritual revolution was still on. Yes, there was magic in life. I told him about my trip to see Baba. I told him about the work that I was doing at the UN to introduce Prout. I reminded him that he was a spiritual revolutionary and that he should never forget it. God would use him as God saw fit, if Dean would let him.

Over breakfast, Greg was mostly quiet, nodding agreement with my assertions. When we parted company, we told each other let's not be strangers. We needed each other to keep the faith.

A couple of months later I received another call from Greg. He told me that Dean had left Denver. He had given his wife the house, the car, all his possessions and was now staying with Greg.

Dean's decisive action had sparked something in Greg and Scott. They wanted to know if I would consider coming to Washington DC for a weekend to strategize how we could collectively recommit ourselves to our spiritual mission. I agreed to come.

Greg, Dean, Scott, and Elaine met me at the train station on the following Friday night. We went out to eat and talked about Baba and our days together in Carbondale.

Elaine was originally from Carbondale too, although she had been living in Brooklyn for many years. I had seen her once or twice when mutual friends would come into town but we weren't close. Apparently, Dean had called her after leaving Denver and asked her to join us. I never knew it, but there was clearly something going on between them. They were like kids together, laughing and cracking jokes. They teamed up to do an imitation of a farty old New York Jewish couple that brought us to tears. Dean was Jewish. Elaine was a natural born comedian. She described herself as part Swiss and part white trash. Her father, who was Swiss, left her mother when Elaine was a baby. Elaine grew up in the back seat of a Chevy with her two sisters, as her mom meandered her way through the old South. Mom was a raucous alcoholic, who went from man to man, but loved her kids and managed to keep things minimally together as they careened from here to there.

Elaine was good looking, vivacious, gutsy, and had an infectious laugh. She had been working for a real estate company selling condos to people. She was doing alright for herself.

Elaine had not been a disciple of Baba Anandamurti, but as we talked over dinner, I could see she was open to a spiritual adventure. Little did any of us know what God had in store for her. As we told our stories and bared our inner truths, she seemed to fit right in.

Scott was another story. He was a good looking, extremely competent, self-possessed, and a highly paid, super attorney. His company flew him around the world to put mergers and acquisitions together. He normally worked sixty to eighty hours a week. We looked at Scott like he was dancing with the devil. His reasoning, however, was that so long as he could keep his meditation together, he was still his own man. There was no doubt that Scott was brilliant,but as for understanding the negative social consequences of his work, he wasn't that aware.

The next morning, we had a leisurely breakfast and then went for a hike in the woods that ran through Washington DC. When we returned to Greg's, we meditated and had a quick lunch. In the afternoon we were sitting on the floor in Greg's living room making our plans. We couldn't quite put our finger on anything yet, but we were committed to a process. We talked about forming a consulting company of some kind. Because Dean was free, he was given the task to firm something up for us. Scott and Greg agreed to support Dean in this phase. We knew that we had access to Washington DC, the capitol of the United States and to New York City, the capitol of the world. My work at the United Nations would certainly be factored into the plans.

In the late afternoon our discussion was interrupted by a phone call that Greg answered. It was Clark Sutton. Clark was the Office Secretary for the Prout sectoral headquarters in Washington DC. He did not know that we were meeting. He had called to give Greg some tragic news. We watched Greg's face go slack. When he hung up, he turned to us and said "Baba's dead."

We bombarded Greg with a thousand worthless questions for which he had no answers. What he learned from Clark, he told us. Baba had been giving the monks around him warnings for the last few days. He was giving them subtle hints that he was going to leave his body, but no one believed him. It wasn't the right time. I don't think there was a person among us who didn't expect Baba to live into the next millennium. Baba knew otherwise. He had been resting in his room. When he didn't respond to his routine schedule, his doctors were called. They pronounced him dead last night. The organization was holding a cremation ceremony at Tiljala in four days. In Washington DC at 7:00 p.m., there was going to be a local meditation at the Ananda Marga center. That was it. That's all Greg knew.

Our father was gone. The light of our lives, the reason for our being was snuffed out as mysteriously as he had come into our lives. It just couldn't be. It couldn't be.

We didn't say much to each other after this, but to hear about Baba's passing in this way, when we had all come together to commit ourselves to his work, gave greater poignancy to our meeting.

At the evening get-together we all meditated. The energy in the room was turbulent and meditation was punctuated with tears and cries. Afterward, we sat in a circle and talked about what this meant to each of us. Many of us, including myself, were in complete denial. When it came my turn to speak, I told people that I did not believe that Baba had died. I thought it was a test of our devotion and commitment to his mission. Just as Baba had brought me back to life in that dingy airport in Calcutta by telling me to sit up and do my spiritual practices, I now implored Baba to do the same. I was in a heady, frightened state of love, anger, and confusion. I hoped against hope that Baba would hear my plea.

A week later at the cremation ceremony that the Margiis called "Mayaprayan" —the Great Passing, my interpretation of events was proven wrong. Baba had left his body. It was cremated in the midst of tens of thousands of people. The organization plunged into a dark sea of grief and confusion.

I didn't go to India for the ceremony. I couldn't bear to go back there without him. I went to work instead, but found myself leaving work early a few days running. I found myself wandering aimlessly through the city until I came upon a church. I'd go inside sick with misery and try to meditate. When I couldn't sit any longer, I'd wander around again until I'd find another church and do the same thing. Shaam and Jan were patient with me. Shaam told me, however that I had to pull myself together—that if Baba was who I believed he was, he was still with us in spirit and nothing had really changed. It wasn't what I wanted to hear, but I knew that he was right. Funny how it took Shaam the atheist to set me straight.

All in all, our little life raft survived the storm intact. Within a couple of weeks, Dean had moved to New York and was now staying with Elaine in Brooklyn. After a few more weeks, I left Commercial*ARTS*. Dean and I now began to put together a nonprofit consulting firm we called The Progress Agency.

Taking advantage of my contacts at the UN and our Proutist interpretation of international political-economy, we framed our mission, goals, and strategic plan. Our chief objective was to put Prout theory into the nucleus of the *sustainable development* paradigm as it was being formed in debates occurring at the United Nations. Sustainable Development, which meant *development that meets the needs of the present without compromising the ability of future generations to meet their own needs,* was beginning to challenge the status quo of capitalist and communist ideologies.

As we sought to fulfill our objective, our work led to us establishing relations with personnel from United Nations departments and international development organizations. Eventually, it led to a meeting with a representative of a seven hundred year old Sufi dynasty centered in Dhaka, Bangladesh. Sufis are Muslim mystics, organized in schools, each established over time by a great spiritual master. Each school carries a rich lineage, often characterized by crossover allegiances as schools adopt the teachings and spiritual practices of other masters into their own liturgy and spiritual practices. Hazrat Shah Sufi Sayed Dayemullah, or Huzur, as he was reverently called, was purportedly such a spiritual master. His school (Tariqat) was called the Dayera Sharif and it was located in the heart of old Dhaka. The Dayera Sharif was linked to four other great lineages that could be traced back to the Prophet Mohammed himself. The issue for us was that Huzur was not a disembodied master, but, in fact, a master in the flesh, who we later learned had been intently watching our little venture from afar.

There is a connection between Baba Anandamurti and Huzur that few others know about. They have come with the same message to humanity at a time when the carrier wave of human evolution —industrial civilization itself—stands on the brink of its own destruction. When it fails, all of humanity will face challenges, hardships, and horrors undreamed of. The human species might not even survive, or if it does, the survivors could be thrown back into the dark ages. The masters came at this moment to provide humanity with guidelines for getting through the social collapse and for establishing a post-capitalist society.

Let me begin by saying that the dynamics that drive the world political economy are not those that are portrayed on CBS or other mainstream capitalist news media. I can say this because through our work at the UN and through the Progress Agency, we saw firsthand what the dynamics are. Unfortunately, most people, particularly Americans, have no idea what course we are traversing, nor what consequences we can expect. It's as Buckminster Fuller used to say, 'people don't get out of the way of what they don't see coming.'

At the beginning of the 1990s, just as the Progress Agency was coming into being, the UN was struggling through an internal upheaval that was triggered by an in-house publication called *Our Common Future*.[5] This book was produced by the United Nation's World Commission on Environment and Development. To understand the significance of this upheaval and why the Masters chose to incarnate at this time in human events, it is necessary to understand certain things about the United Nations because it is the only human institution composed of representatives from every nation on earth whose work it is to address the broader issues of human existence.

The UN was set up after World War II under the leadership of the US government in order to formalize the new era of Pax Americana. Europe had been decimated by the war and the seat of capitalism now moved to the US.

David Rockefeller, the supreme architect of American capitalism and the primary instigator of the global economy in which we now find ourselves, donated land on the East River in Manhattan

---

5   The World Commission on Environment and Development, *Our Common Future* (New York: Oxford University Press, 1987).

to construct the UN Headquarters. The Security Council was established with five nations holding permanent seats, the US, England, France, China, and Russia. The Security Council was given primary responsibility for the maintenance of *international peace and security*. Under the Charter, all Member States are obligated to comply with Council decisions. In some cases, the Security Council has the authority to impose economic sanctions or authorize the use of force to maintain or restore international peace and security.

Russia had been an ally against the Nazis and other fascists in the Second World War, but soon after the war ended, it became the major enemy of the US as it sought to institute a communist world. The dynamics of the Cold War were crafted in the maneuverings and chess-like strategies within the Security Council. Needless to say, the capitalist countries were the dominant power and controlled the decision-making in the Security Council.

A different dynamic, however, developed in the UN General Assembly. Here, every member state had equal representation and the focus was not explicitly centered on security issues and *real politik*.

During the 1950s, the General Assembly concentrated on defining *human rights*. It was a reasonably harmless exercise that allowed nations to get to know each other. By focusing on values, the contentious issue of political-economy that divided the capitalist and communist world was side-stepped.

By putting reality aside for several years, the General Assembly produced the UN Universal Declaration of Human Rights. In one sense, the Declaration changed nothing. Governments behaved the same after the release of the document as they did before. Yet, in another sense, the document provided stark evidence that human beings the world over hold the same values. Everyone wants the opportunity to meet their basic needs in a peaceful environment and to be treated with dignity and respect by those in authority and by other nations.

As *values* provided the focus for General Assembly deliberations in the 1950s, *politics* became the focus for the 1960s. This occurred because European countries could no longer maintain their far-flung empires and were engaged in the process of decolonization. Throughout the Far East, Middle East, Africa, and Latin America, new nation-states were being born every year and joined the United Nations as members. While the people of these nation-states were exhilarated with the flush of freedom, they were left without administrative structures with which to govern themselves. The task of training the new, home-grown bureaucrats in the theory and practice of democratic capitalism fell to the United Nations.

In the 1970s, the focus of the General Assembly shifted again as the growing number of new countries gained a stronger voice. Now a bloc of "non-aligned" nations arose, who identified neither with the capitalist, nor the communist systems. They were called the "Group of 77" to indicate the number of countries that constituted its original membership. As the years passed, more and more countries joined the non-aligned movement, eventually constituting a majority of the human race.

This new "third world," by virtue of the *one nation, one vote* rule of the General Assembly, gained predominance and began to set the agenda of the Assembly in the 1970s. By now, they realized that political freedom was a hollow victory at best, without economic freedom. They could make all the political pronouncements they wanted, but in reality, their resource base was still "owned" by foreign corporations. Profits from their industrial base were still siphoned off to distant lands instead of being reinvesting in the local infrastructure to meet the basic needs of local people and improve their lot.

The new capitalist order of Pax Americana was more subtle than European Imperialism, but it meant the same economic slavery for the people who were exploited. If local political leaders spoke out against the oppression of their people, they were silenced. If they could not be bought, they were killed. If they could not be killed, domestic and international opposition was raised against them until they broke or were destroyed. In the meantime, local eco-systems were ravaged and millions, then billions, of people were left to wallow in dire poverty.

In the 1970s, the leaders of the non-aligned nations, under the protection of greater numbers and polite UN protocols, introduced an alternative economic plan in the General Assembly called the "New Economic Order." When stripped of its verbiage, the plan came down to a complaint about how the corporations were destroying the environment and the social fabric of their countries and called for better trade agreements between the "developing" and the "industrial" countries.

Russia supported the plan, but had no power to change economic conditions. The capitalist governments, for their part, stone-walled the issue even as disconcerting evidence mounted regarding environmental degradation and the ticking *population bomb* triggered by abject poverty.

Eventually, in the early 1980s, a plenary meeting was scheduled between the leaders of the third world on the tenets of the New Economic Order. Once the meeting began, however, deliberations faltered immediately over the question of who would be the arbiter of last resort, that is, who would have the last word. The third world leaders wanted the discussions to be held as part of the General Assembly deliberations, because they obviously held a majority in this body. The capitalists, for their part wanted the World Bank, where they held power, to be the venue for discussions. It was an impasse that could not be breached and it killed the discussions before they could begin.

Typically, when political powers don't want to address issues that they believe will undermine their power, they appoint a commission to further study the issue. This is also what happened now. The World Commission on Environment and Development (WCED) was set up in 1983 to reexamine the environmental and economic development problems on the planet and to formulate realistic proposals to address them.

Gro Bruntland, the former President of Norway, was chosen to head the Commission. Its composition was well-balanced between the major political power blocks. The G-7 (capitalists), OPEC (Middle Eastern oil powers), the Soviet Bloc, and the Group of 77 (non-aligned nations) were all represented.

The initial meetings of the Commission were characterized by raucous finger-pointing. The third world members attacked the capitalists for sucking their countries dry and for causing wide scale impoverishment and environmental degradation. The capitalists retaliated by charging the third world leaders with administrative and fiscal incompetence and for letting their populations grow too large to be sustainable.

Things began to settle down when the Commissioners traveled to each continent to take a look for themselves as to the state of affairs. In addition to their sightseeing, they collected a mountain of scientific data and also listened to testimonies of local people in prearranged "town hall" meetings set up to gain input from local people.

After a couple of years of this, a clearer picture of the state of the world began to emerge. The Commissioners published their findings in 1987 in the small book called *Our Common Future*. It proved to be a bombshell, in part because its findings were unanimously agreed upon, and secondly because of what it said.

Our Common Future changed the planetary dialogue and set the stage for United Nations deliberations into the foreseeable future.

In one fell swoop, it blew away the importance of the ideological debate concerning capitalism and communism and replaced it with a new ideological framework called "sustainable development." The book reminded us that the world scientific community continued to call our attention to urgent and complex environmental problems which called human survival into question—problems like global warming, ozone deterioration, desertification, and the loss of species and forests, along with potable water and arable soil. It criticized the governments of the industrialized world for not responding to these problems and for dodging their responsibility by absently calling for more details and by assigning the problem to institutions unequipped to cope with or provide solutions to the problems.

It reaffirmed that the majority of human beings living in poor countries are caught in "a downward spiral of linked ecological and economic decline." This linkage between economic activity and environmental consequences was an important first step in understanding the human condition. The book stated "the environment is where we all live, and development is what we all do in attempting to improve our lot within that abode."[6]

In this book, the term *sustainable development* was coined as "meeting the needs of the present without compromising the ability of future generations to meet their own needs."[7] *Our Common Future* galvanized the international community and caused the General Assembly to call for a series of global summit meetings to address the declining social and environmental conditions facing humanity. The first of these was the United Nations Conference on Environment and Development held in Rio de Janeiro in 1992. Popularly called the *Earth Summit*, it brought together all the world's governments as well as twenty-five thousand people's organizations from around the world to look at how to solve our common problems.

Let it be said that, at this point, no matter how the world had been cowed and lulled to sleep by the capitalist corporations, governments, and media, humanity awoke for a brief moment in 1992 and saw its house on fire. And though it still remains cowed by repressive states and stupefied by blind consumerism, humanity is having trouble going back to sleep. The events that transpired at the UN and the world summits can never be undone and the spiritual Master's role on this stage will continue to unfold because its purpose is to guide us in the process of human revolution.

The Progress Agency

Dean cut a deal with Steve Kliegerman, who was the owner of the real estate company where Elaine worked. The deal allowed the Progress Agency to have an office in exchange for Dean providing sales training for Steve's staff. The office was located in Manhattan at One West Union Square Park, overlooking the corner of the park with the Mahatma Gandhi statue.

During the first few months of the Progress Agency, we attended UN briefings every Thursday morning and met a wide range of people. We sponsored a couple of forums at the Church Center which was the non-profit headquarters located across 1st Avenue from the UN. At the forums, we introduced the core ideas of *Progressive Development*. This was the term Dean and I created to describe our writings at the Progress Agency. It was a blend of *Prout* and *sustainable development* that put human values at the core of the economic and environmental analysis that characterized sustainable development. In our writings and presentations, we agreed that it was a large step for governments to vocalize the link between environmental degradation and economic activity, as *Our Common Future* had done. Yet, we argued, that economy and environment were only two spokes of a wheel that required a much greater analysis of current reality. We drew a chart to illustrate our point.

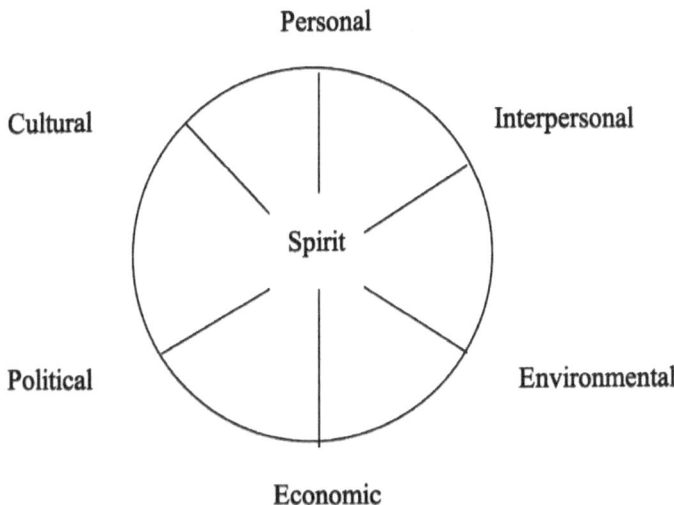

We postulated that human beings operate in several arenas at once, personal, interpersonal, political, economic, cultural and environmental. Therefore, a universal paradigm should account for these arenas in order to optimize human advancement and protect the natural world.

We made it clear, that Spirit is not just another spoke on the wheel that competed with other activities for our attention. It wasn't a matter of should I go to the office or should I go to church on Sunday morning. Rather Spirit (pure consciousness) was the ground of being that provided the nuclear impetus for all of life. It was

Consciousness, not matter, from which all forms emerged and, as such, provided the foundation for morality, cooperation and unity.

The world cannot exist without Spirit, just as a wheel cannot exist without a hub. As human beings, we need to understand this truth. To continue to believe that matter is the summum bonum of human existence, as even sustainable development was want to do, will only lead to more competition and divisiveness. Humanity could more easily meet its basic needs through cooperation rather than the dog-eat-dog competition that characterized global capitalism. The true purpose of the state, religions, and other social institutions is not to control our behavior or simply provide defense or welfare. Rather, it is to assist each individual to reach his or her highest potential, i.e., to become self-realized.

As for the economy, if it was to exist to optimize human potential, it could not be about making profit for a few, but about meeting the basic needs of all. In addition, it needed to preserve the ecosystems of the planet. The environment is not simply *raw materials* or a container for our activity, but also an intrinsic expression of Spirit. As such, its protection is required to advance personal and collective evolution.

The Progress Agency was about building a constituency that supported these values and that would help humanity free itself from poverty and slavery before it was too late.

That being said, at the same time, we also needed to make enough money to pay our bills and keep the ball rolling. There were no corporate or government grants to support our revolutionary ideas. We had to develop clients to make money. Our first big client was Earth Day.

One of the national Earth Day offices was run by a man named Bruce Anderson who operated out of Vermont. Bruce, along with a small staff, created promotional materials and supplied information to organizations around the country on how to create an Earth Day event. For the most part, however, there were local organizations in the bigger cities that controlled their own Earth Day events. We were hired to create a stronger collaborative effort, raise bigger dollars, and develop planning events and a newspaper that would solidify the movement.

While we worked on Earth Day tasks, we also planned for the UN Earth Summit that was scheduled to take place in Rio de Janeiro in June, 1992. We had petitioned for and received permits to participate in the UN Preparatory Conferences that set the agenda for the Earth Summit. We wanted to have a big impact on this event and we concentrated on mobilizing Ananda Marga and Prout organizations to have a strong presence there.

One of the vehicles for introducing the Progress Agency to the UN community was the Communications Coordination Committee of the UN (CCC/UN). This was an organization to which I belonged and for which I edited its bi-monthly newsletter that was circulated to the NGO (non-governmental organization) community affiliated with the UN. The CCC/UN was actually the oldest NGO. Established in 1946, its mission was to help the UN build and coordinate its outreach with the NGO community. At this time, however, it wasn't a particularly influential organization, but it had some progressive people as members. These included Harry Lerner, the propounder of a UN People's Assembly, Lenny Rubin, a business man well connected with the health industry, and Joe Eger, the conductor of the UN symphony orchestra. When the CCC/UN began, there were only a handful of NGOs, now there were over five hundred. Many were large and powerful organizations like the Red Cross, CARE, the Rotary Club, the Chamber of Commerce, etc. The NGOs could be religious organizations, or organizations concerned with trade, relief, development, or any of a myriad of issues, in short, any organization that provided a service to humanity.

The CCC/UN met weekly. In May of 1991, at one of these meetings, I met a man named Nurul Alam. Alam was from Bangladesh. He was the executive director of the Dayemi Complex, the social service component of the Dayera Sharif, a Sufi order that traced its lineage back to the Prophet Mohammed (Upon him be peace).

Alam was a quiet, good looking man with soft features, jet black hair, and a golden cast to his skin. It was the first time that I had seen him at a meeting and afterward we spoke. I told him about the Progress Agency and he told me about the Dayemi Complex in Bangladesh. They had schools and orphanages and agricultural projects. Alam described an organization that I believed could definitely use our consulting services. We exchanged business cards and agreed to meet again. I wanted Dean to meet him.

We met together for lunch a week later in the UN cafeteria, a large carpeted room with good food that overlooked the East River and across the river into Queens. Dean was explaining the benefits of using the Progress Agency and Alam was leaning forward and nodding his head in affirmation. Suddenly Alam pulled his hands in, sat up straight and looked at us intently. "I will work with you," he said, "From this day, I will dedicate two days a week to the Progress Agency." Alam grinned broadly.

Alam told us that he was especially taken by our "Moment of Truth" project. He said that he could ensure the participation of Bangladesh in the event. The Moment of Truth was an inspiration of Dean's that had been incorporated into the Progress Agency work. The idea was to have everyone in the world share a simultaneous moment of silent reflection on the course of social and environmental degradation and collectively commit ourselves to human unity and care of the planet as we entered the new millennium. The event would symbolize the emergence of a species-consciousness committed to a sustainable lifestyle. While it made an interesting metaphor and allowed us to discuss our ideas with new contacts, neither of us saw it as realistically happening. We had neither the labor power nor the money to pull off such an event. Yet here was Alam offering to bring a country to the table, and even saying he would help us introduce it to other Muslim countries. Even so, it wasn't exactly what we were aiming for. We needed a cash paying client. We parted company and Dean and I took the subway back to the office. C'est la vie.

At the end of the week, I was scheduled to go to an Ananda Marga retreat in Missouri. I would be gone for seven days. Dean would hold down the fort. At the retreat, I would meet with Proutists from around the country and tell them about the Progress Agency and our work. There was some resentment that Dean and I hadn't developed our strategy within the organization of Proutist Universal. We had considered doing so, but we realized that we couldn't place our livelihood, as tenuous as it was, in the hands of central workers in India, with whom we would have sporadic communication at best. Consulting was also not a practice within the organization's bylaws. More than this, however, Dean did not want to work within the organization. He had been personally hurt by members of the hierarchy and didn't want to be involved with it. As it was, I had a little fence mending to do and Dean was content to remain in New York.

It was the week of July 4, 1991. I was now in Missouri at the Ananda Marga retreat site just outside Willow Springs. There were about five people at the retreat. The sun was high and the day was hot and humid. We had just finished noon meditation and were going to the cafeteria for lunch when someone approached me to say there was a phone call for me in the office. That's strange, I thought. I sensed an emergency. I hoped it wasn't Ellen calling me.

It was Dean. His voice was uncharacteristically awkward and hesitant.

"What's wrong," I asked.

"Chuck, something's going on. I don't know what to make of it."

"What are you talking about?" I asked attentively.

"It's Alam. I got a call from him on Tuesday. He asked if he could come over to my apartment. He said that he had something to tell me."

According to New York business etiquette, it was most unusual and could be considered poor taste to ask someone to visit their home on a business matter, especially if you just met.

"Well, what did he say?" I demanded.

"I hope you're sitting down, Chuck, because I sure am. Another pause at the other end of the line. "Basically he said that I am the 'Friend of God' for whom his Tariqat has been waiting since it was prophesied over three hundred years ago by a Sufi master in the family's lineage."

My brain seized up. It was as if someone tripped an alarm and all the doors and windows slammed shut and locked. Fragments of questions flooded my brain. Things began to gurgle in my glandular system. I fished for words.

"So why is it exactly that the family has been waiting for you?"

"Alam says I am to bring true Islam to the world."

"True Islam!?"

That's just great, I thought. Dean didn't know anything about Islam. He was Jewish and studied yoga. His name was Greenberg, for God's sake.

"Alam said that by his Master's command he has been searching for me the past seven years in New York City."

There was a long silence.

Finally I said,

"Okay, can we go over this again? Tell me what happened." My brain just couldn't get any traction.

Dean patiently began again.

"Alam asked if he could come to see me at my apartment. He sounded urgent. I invited him over. Elaine was there, Chuck, she can confirm this. He said his Master is a Sufi named Hazrat Shah Sufi Sayed Dayemullah. Alam calls him Huzur. I think it's a term of respect or endearment like Baba. Alam said that Huzur carries the lineage of a Sufi dynasty that dated back to the Prophet Mohammed. Huzur's family are Moguls who settled Dhaka hundreds of years ago. In fact, the guy who first settled in Dhaka was named Sheikh Mohammed Dayem. The Dayera Sharif was named after him. It was he who made the prophesy about the Friend of God coming."

"So what's this have to do with you? You're Jewish. You're a yogi. You don't know anything about Islam."

"I don't know what it has to do with me, Chuck, I'm only telling you what happened." Dean's voice was sober.

"All I know is that, according to Alam, this Sheikh Dayem said the Friend of God would come at this time. He would not be a member of the lineage but he would carry the lineage forward."

"So . . . so wait a minute, does this Huzur want you to be his successor?! Are you going to become a Sheikh . . . a Sufi . . . a Master? Is that what you are telling me?" Is this what Alam believes, that you're the guy?"

"Alam said that he had a vision of me but that it wasn't a clear picture. He said that when he met you he thought that you might be the one from his vision. But when he met me at the UN he knew it was me.

After Alam left us, he called Huzur and Huzur confirmed that he had found the Friend of Allah."

"Holy sh*t!"

"Huzur told Alam several things about me. When Alam came to see me, he recounted these things to me. Chuck, I tell you from the bottom of my heart, nobody could have known some of the things that Alam told me. No research could have revealed my inner most thoughts."

I stood by the desk, my ear to the phone, my composure like a fly hitting a closed window. I was stupefied, mystified, and in pain. Selfishly, I was concerned about what this would do to our little fledgling Progress Agency. I was worried for my livelihood.

"What now?" I finally asked Dean.

"Alam says that Huzur wants to see me as soon as I can arrange to go to Bangladesh." "They said they will handle all my expenses," Dean hurriedly added.

"Oh," I said.

"Chuck, I had to call and tell you this. I didn't think it could wait for your return."

"Yes, of course."

"Chuck do you think I should go?"

"You have to go. You have no choice," I said quietly.

Dean spent most of the summer in Bangladesh. While he was gone, I busied myself designing our corporate ID materials, developing a fundraising letter, and writing the Progress Agency's first newsletter. I also worked on a couple of graphics projects for clients and tried, mostly unsuccessfully, to keep the Earth Day project moving.

Money was still a large worry. Apparently, my faith in God only stretched so far despite the miracles I had witnessed—despite the love and attention I had been paid. While I had about one year's expenses covered due to my savings and my settlement with Commercial*ARTS*, I also had a new baby to feed. My son, Chris, was born on January 18, 1990. Another constant pressure that had resulted from my sudden change of occupation and uncertain money stream was that Ellen became extremely anxious and this drove a wedge between us.

Ellen characterized the situation as one in which I was conned by Dean, a fast talking interloper who came into town and threw our whole life up for grabs. She lost faith in me now, demanding to know how I could become such a weak-minded "follower" bent on self-destruction. Dean had Elaine to support him. Who would support me? Dean could afford to take risks. I couldn't. Ellen despised Dean and I found myself wrenched by split loyalties. When Ellen asked what I did at work each day, it was like being interrogated by the Grand Inquisitor. Each day that passed without financial stability made me guiltier in Ellen's eyes. My self-assuredness began to waver.

Had I leapt into the fire without thinking? Could I realistically dedicate myself to a spiritual mission and support a family at the same time? I was in uncharted waters without models to follow. I had only my faith in my master and constant anxiety to guide me.

One evening I had dinner with an old friend, Bill Elson. We had gone to Illinois Benedictine College together and had kept in touch by having dinner together once or twice a year. Bill ran the music division for an international entertainment agency called ICM Partners. He had either managed or booked, at one time or another, some of the greatest rock and roll stars of our day—Janice Joplin, the Jefferson Airplane, Paul McCartney, and Ozzie Osborne had all been clients of Bill. Bill was a pragmatic, somewhat cynical, "had it up to here with the exotic" kind of guy. I told him my story over dinner because I wanted to see if I was certifiable crazy from a professional, business-like point of view. He listened intently to my story, sat back in his chair, shook his head and said, "You're a lot braver man than I am." That was it. I'll be darned. He didn't think I was crazy. He didn't dismiss me or call me a fool. He just couldn't figure out how I could throw myself into the flames on the strength of my beliefs.

If the truth were known, however, it wasn't bravery that made me go into partnership with Dean. I told you what happened. What would you call it? I just *had* to do it. I didn't think about the consequences. I was the fool stepping blithely off a cliff, knowing in my heart that my Father would catch me. I still believed this. It's just that I didn't realized how terrifying a free fall could be or how a vision of my own crash could fill me with such dread.

When Dean went to Bangladesh, he arranged to have some people join him after a month. Elaine went along with Scott Hudgeons and two other guys, Michael Wyman and Larry Greenwald. Larry was a friend of Dean's from Denver who had volunteered to be the accountant of the Progress Agency. Michael was someone we had met at the UN. He was a short, chunky guy who dressed nicely and was always sweating. He was very funny and had a special knack for getting people to *acknowledge* each other. Michael organized interpersonal relations workshops. In these workshops, he would tell people that they were spiritual beings, brothers and sisters who knew each other deep inside if they only bothered to take a look. Michael ran a session at a Progress Agency forum and it was quite remarkable. While he chattered on about who we *really* were, joking and being buoyant, he lined us up in two lines so that we stood facing each other about a foot apart. We now had to keep looking into the other person's eyes until we found who we were looking for—our brother or sister. After a few minutes of looking intently into another person's eyes, with Michael stopping by to put his hands on our shoulders and telling us how incredible the other person was, total strangers broke down crying and told their partners that they loved them. It was most amazing. Talk about a great ice-breaker for a meeting! That's not to say that this *love* lasted much longer than the exercise, but people did get in touch with something that opened their hearts and kept them open for some time.

Michael understood something about the human spirit. He had a gift, but he wasn't a spiritual person. Michael just loved life. He was more of an epicurean. He ate and drank feverishly and wanted to feel good as much as possible. The only thing that slowed Michael down was the need to make money. Dean took Michael to Bangladesh because Michael loved us; he was fun to be around and; he was looking for an adventure.

The journey to Bangladesh proved to be quite incredible. Elaine, Scott, and even Michael confirmed that Huzur was a true spiritual master and that, indeed, he had treated Dean as his long-lost son. Everywhere they traveled throughout Bangladesh, Huzur now introduced Dean as Din Mohammed Abdullah, the friend of Allah. They said that children waved flags at Dean's coming and ran after his car, shouting his name.

As amazing as this was to hear, I was more fascinated by learning of an event that put Elaine in the center of attention. While the event itself was awe provoking, it was even more remarkable because it took place in a Muslim country where women are literally not seen, nor heard. This is what happened.

The small entourage arrived in Bangladesh at the time when the Dayera Sharif was holding its annual commemoration of the death of Huzur's father, Sheik Azmatullah. Like Huzur, he was also a Sufi master, revered and renowned throughout Bangladesh. Each year, Imams and devotees from all over Bangladesh came to honor him at an event that lasted several days and was usually attended by over ten thousand people.

It was the evening of the first day's activities. The event was held at Ibrahimpur, a rural project of the Dayemi Sharif, a couple of hours outside of Dhaka. A large tent had been hoisted and thousands of men were packed inside. On the stage sat a great semi-circle of Imams with black and white shawls over their heads. Huzur sat at the center of the arc, in the center of the stage.

There were no women in the tent. According to hundreds of years of tradition, it was forbidden for the women to enter a holy gathering of this nature. Where were the women? They were separated by several rows of shabby curtains, out in the field cooking food for the night's dinner.

Due to the *generosity* of the men, however, they were graced by being allowed to listen to the speeches and activities in the tent over an old, squawk box speaker hooked up to a microphone on the stage.

The congregation had been informed that Dean was the *Friend of Allah* and was to be the Chief Guest at the weeklong assembly. He was to speak to the crowd this evening and introduce the Moment of Truth. It was expected that everyone would take a pledge to abide by the values of the Moment of Truth and work together in the spirit of unity. Huzur was to take the oath as well.

When Dean and the others arrived that evening at Ibrahimpur, they entered the rear of the giant tent and walked to the front. As they approached the stage, the men began to fawn over Dean, but others became outraged that he had brought a woman into the tent. Elaine was quickly approached by several scowling men who promptly escorted her back and out of the tent. Dean, who had his eyes solely focused on the slight frame of Huzur, in the middle of the stage, did not notice what had transpired behind him.

Michael and Scott were escorted to a place in the front row facing the stage. Dean was escorted onto the stage. He greeted Huzur in the traditional Sufi fashion by saying "As'Salaamu Alaykum (May peace be upon you)" with his hand over his heart. He knelt and sat back on his legs in front of the master and bent down to touch the hem of his garment. Then they embraced. Huzur offered Dean a seat on his right side.

Once seated Dean immediately realized that Elaine was no longer with him. Where had she gone? He looked to Scott and Michael. They signaled back that she had been taken away. What? Michael and Scott hunched their shoulders. Yeah.

Now I ask you, what would you have done in this situation? You are a stranger in a strange land. You do not understand the customs of the place. You are surrounded by thousands of men, with centuries of tradition telling you that your girlfriend has to stay outside with the rest of the women. And you are sitting center stage beside a perfect master in a ring of Muslim Imams. Nobody cares about Elaine. All eyes are on the Great One who has been telling people that you are his successor. And you are a white, Jewish boy from Peoria, Illinois in a country that is ninety percent Muslim. Would you make a scene about it or would you just let it go?

Dean immediately arose and left the tent looking for Elaine. He was told that she had been taken to a small tent out back. Dean found her. When she told him what had happened, he decided to stay with her in the little tent.

Elaine was alarmed. She told Dean to go back to the tent. He was the Chief Guest. It's no big thing. She understood tradition. Dean says simply that he would not go back without her. When messengers are sent to find him, he tells them the same thing. He will not go back without Elaine.

Dean's departure is now creating quite a stir in the main tent. Where had the *mystery man* gone? Why had the guest of honor disappeared? Word had been circulating for weeks that Huzur was severing a tradition that reached back to the seventh century to announce that he was choosing Dean as his successor. Never before had the spiritual mantle left the family, never had it left Bangladesh since Huzur's ancestors had settled the area centuries before. Rumors were rife and the tent was filled with expectation and concern. Everyone wanted to see this mysterious stranger from America and listen to his words. Many men had a lifetime of devotion at stake.

Dean would not return to the stage that night. When this was reported, there was an immediate uproar in the tent and even the Imams could not contain themselves. They began a feverish condemnation of Dean's sacrilegious behavior. A few timidly suggested that there was nothing in the Koran that challenged Dean's actions.

Even though the tent was filled with rancor and confusion, the night ended without resolution. Neither did Dean return on the second day. The situation cast a debilitating pall over the event.

On the third day, Huzur, in his croaking voice, addressed the crowd and the tent fell silent. He told the Imams and the multitude that Dean was the *Friend of Allah* and the guest of honor. He said that there was nothing in the Koran to forbid Elaine joining the assembly. The Koran stands for equality and unity between men and women. He told everyone that this was his event and that Elaine was welcome. Moreover, he would ask Elaine to address the gathering. The place was struck dumb. A messenger was again sent and this time he returned with Dean and Elaine. Dean sat at Huzur's right side and Elaine sat at Dean's right side. The sight of this big blond white woman sitting at the center of the ring of Imam's was mesmerizing. The fact that no man's eyes had ever seen such a sight was compounded by the fact that no man's father's eyes, or grandfather's eyes, or great grandfather's eyes, or for that matter any Muslim man's eyes throughout history and the world had ever seen such a sight.

Now Huzur reminded the congregation of the three hundred year old prophecy that spoke of Dean's coming and he told everyone that he had been guided by Allah to recognize Dean as the one who was foretold. Huzur declared to one and all that Dean had come to bring *true Islam* to the world. Despite the trepidation that roiled the crowd of men, everyone now knew that the situation was serious and that history was being made, and no matter whether they accepted it or not, they were witness to it.

Huzur now invited Dean to speak. Dean began by greeting the multitude *"As'Salaamu Alaykum"* May the peace of Allah be upon you.

The tent responded *"Wa Alaykum Salaam."* And also upon your spirit.

Dean had it in him to offer a two-hour homily no sweat. This, in fact, is what the crowd expected. This was the appropriate thing to do to establish himself as a teacher. But Dean did not do this. Instead, he introduced Elaine and said that she would speak to them in his place. He sat down and prodded Elaine to get up. She was caught completely off guard.

The crowd buzzed and rattled and Elaine closed her eyes to compose herself. She arose slowly and took a couple of steps forward. She glanced back at Dean and he nodded encouragement. She looked at Huzur. His face was impassive. When she turned back around, she gazed into a sea of men's faces as far as she could see. To her left and to her right, all around her nothing but the faces of men.

"As'Salaamu Alaykum"

"Wa Alaykum Salaam"

Dead silence. Elaine began to speak softly into the microphone. She told the men that like them, she was here only by Allah's grace. It was not her intention to make them angry or to defy their traditions.

She told them that she was not a Muslim or a Sufi and that if she violated their customs she was heartily sorry and asked for their forgiveness.

In New York, she said, she had met people from many religions. There are many religions on earth and they each have their own customs and traditions. She told the men that when she met people, she was not so much concerned about the trappings of their religion but how they reflected goodness—how they treated their fellow human beings, the creatures of the earth, and the earth itself.

She said that to her Allah was the name for the Oneness, the Divine Consciousness. Allah existed in all things. "Isn't this so?" she asked. The men murmured their assent.

Allah exists in women, just as he does in men, she continued. She had read about great women saints like Rabe'ah, Sha'wana, and Mama 'Esmat Tabrizi who were Sufis and who had a personal, miraculous relationship with Allah. Wasn't this true?

Then Elaine, still with great humility, but as she was wanted to do, addressed the issue head-on. "I believe," she said, "that the act of suppressing women by not allowing them to sit with men during spiritual meetings is an act that is validated by custom and tradition only, but not by the Koran." There was an audible gasp, followed by angry outcries. The air became explosive. The audacity of this female *kafir*!

She continued bravely. "In the Koran it was Khadijah, the wife of the Prophet Mohammed (Upon him be peace) who protected him during his early days. It was Khadijah who believed in him when no others did, who lovingly consoled him, telling him that he was not crazy for having his visions. Wasn't it true that in the days when the Prophet was the most vulnerable that it was a woman who nurtured him until his faith was strong enough to carry him forward to meet his destiny?"

Now the air was literally crackling. Shouts were going up everywhere. Some men had risen to their feet. The din was awesome. Yet, while some men were incensed by her audacity, others were in tears, believing that they were listening to a great saint. An upheaval was occurring in the hearts of men.

Elaine concluded by asking their forgiveness. In all the noise, however, it was unlikely that the men heard her final words.

Something else was now happening that stole their attention. Over their own noise and shouting, an even greater, higher pitched noise was swelling. At first no one knew what was happening. It was a noise coming from outside the tent. As the men stopped to listen, the noise got louder—a shrill sound, like a million birds calling simultaneously to declare their territory. It got louder and closer. The back flaps of the tent suddenly blasted open and to everyone's shock and amazement a rush of women came running into the tent. Guards immediately began to beat the women with sticks and yelled for them to leave the tent.

Elaine, still at the microphone, shouted at them "Stop that. Stop that. Stop beating the women." Now the entire place was on its feet. Elaine ran off the stage, down the center aisle, back through rows and rows of men, with Dean in pursuit. She threw her body between the guards and the women. She yelled at the stupefied guards and guided the women back outside the tent. Once outside the women surrounded her. They were weeping for joy, yelling, singing, reaching to touch her clothing, her face, her hands, her feet, telling her they loved her, talking to her, blessing her, blessing her in words she could not understand. It was true Islam. I can vouch for this event because I heard the story from many witnesses and saw the photos of Elaine dressed in white surrounded by a large sea of women. Someone had taken them from above, perhaps from a branch of a tree.

Inside the tent, it was announced that the program was over for the afternoon. Dinner would be served after prayer.

The Loaves and Fishes Thing

As Elaine stayed with the women, Huzur and Dean walked together around the grounds. Huzur told Dean that this memorial event for his father brought many people together. Many were not Sufis, but they revered his father as a great saint and came each year to the memorial service. Huzur did not discuss Elaine's homily, but Dean knew that he was not displeased.

As they continued their walk, they approached the place where the women were preparing the food. Dean was immediately struck by the fact that there were only ten or so large pots with fires under them. He felt compelled to mention to Huzur that not enough food was being prepared to feed the large gathering. Huzur raised his eyebrows. This would be inexcusable to not have sufficient food for the guests. Dean reasoned that with only ten pots, each would have to feed more than a thousand people. Clearly an impossibility. Huzur nodded thoughtfully. He stepped over to the pots and blessed them and they continued their walk.

Dean told me how he later watched in amazement as the ladles dipped continuously into the pots until thousands of people were fed and yet there was food to spare that went to the poor in the nearby village.

"He did the loaves and fishes thing, Chuck," Dean solemnly told me.

Traveling With the Master

For the remainder of their time in Bangladesh, Huzur took everyone on a grand tour of the country. They stopped at Dayemi Complex land-based projects, schools, and orphanages, as well as mosques and shrines and other sacred places. At all these places, Elaine was admitted at the Master's behest. Most of them were places in which no woman had ever set foot. At one point, Dean confronted Huzur about the way that women were treated as inferiors in Bangladesh.

Even the Dayemi Complex had no orphanages for girl children. "I think we should open an orphanage for girls," Dean asserted.

"I think it's a good idea," Huzur said, as if surprised that he had not thought of it before.

When Dean told me this story, it made us realize how even Masters are circumscribed by the time, place, and people in their environment. It was only Dean and Elaine's coming that allowed Huzur to teach a valuable lesson about the dignity of women to his followers and countrymen. Such a lesson could be taught in no other way.

While everyone enjoyed the trip, Huzur made it a point to meet with Dean every day continuing to teach him the history, language, customs, rituals, and prayers of Islam. He also did something unexpected one afternoon. He prayed over Dean and repeatedly blew on the top of his head. Afterward, he made Dean stand. Huzur grabbed him in a certain way to adjust his back. Dean said it was the most amazing thing. He said he felt his back "clunk into place."

At another session Huzur taught Dean about the curative power of herbs and ointments, and gave him silver rings and silver pendants that had handwritten prayers folded inside them and sealed with wax. He told Dean that he now had the power to heal people and that he should make this part of his spiritual work.

"Heal people! What does that mean?" I asked Dean. "Does that mean you can cure cancer and things like that?"

Dean was quiet and almost embarrassed. "I don't know what it means, Chuck. I'm just telling you what Huzur said. If I have the power to heal people, it's certainly not my power."

Dean returned to New York in time to see our best client, Earth Day, crash and burn. Before he had left he had been made the CEO of Earth Day. He had presided over a national council composed of representatives from the larger cities. Unfortunately, there were two powerful people on the council, one from New York City, the other from LA who reveled in political intrigue and who wanted to dominate the council for their own purposes. They sought to destroy the new unity of local organizations in order to maintain their own positions as local powers in themselves. During Dean's absence, which admittedly was not in the best interest of Earth Day, they worked behind the scenes to convince Bruce Anderson, the President of Earth Day, who originally had hired Dean, to dismiss Dean as CEO, as well as relinquish his own power and make the council the preeminent decision maker. They argued that this would be the truly democratic thing to do. Bruce fell prey to the trap, trying to keep the peace, but once they had achieved their ends, they railroaded the council into division and inaction. Things fell apart.

As 1992 dawned, we focused on the Earth Summit. This event was important for all the political reasons that were previously mentioned. We felt that the planet was at stake and that we were entering a global dialogue that would shape human destiny. Our contribution to the process was to interject a universal value system into the dialogue, the ideology given to us by P. R. Sarkar, Baba.

It was vitally important that the Progress Agency participate in this event. From a business perspective, it would be a giant trade fair in which we could market our services. From an ideological point of view, it was important that the ideas of the spiritual masters be introduced to the world.

I spent a good amount of time corresponding with monks and nuns from around the world about the registration procedure with the United Nations and the organizers of the People's Forum. This forum, organized for nonprofits, by nonprofits, was to run parallel with the Earth Summit. We would address the same issues that would be addressed by the national governments and create position papers to be shared with the governments.

I worked with the Proutists in Brazil who would be our hosts and arrange for our lodging and food. They would also organize the Prout booth at the People's Forum. We anticipated that about seventy-five organizers would come from around the world to represent our activities. As I worked with Baba's organizations, Dean worked with Alam to involve the Dayemi Complex in the Earth Summit. As a result of Dean's work, we received an invitation from Huzur for the Progress Agency to organize a conference in Dhaka that would be hosted by the Dayera Sharif. The objective of the conference would be to inform the people of Bangladesh about the Earth Summit and gain input from them into the global dialogue on saving the planet.

This was, in fact, an amazing offer. If what Dean said was true, Huzur was connected to the entire country—government, unions, NGOs. Who knew what would come of this. In any case, I would also now have an opportunity to meet Huzur for myself.

As we prepared for the Earth Summit and our trip to Bangladesh, it was becoming apparent to me that Dean was going through a spiritual transformation at amazing speed. The spiritual transformation that normal people go through by virtue of meditation, selfless service, prayer, and their struggle to put God in the center of their lives can't be observed with the naked eye, because it may take months, years, even a life time. By contrast, I was now watching my friend and partner leap years of development in a few months of time. His prayer and meditation became fixed constants in his day. He rose before dawn each morning to do Salat, the Moslem prayer ritual, and practiced it five times a day. In addition, he meditated twice a day, as required by Baba's spiritual system. He had also begun quietly and innocuously to test his powers as a healer. People began to report that Dean had relieved their pain and suffering. One man had a congenital disease that wracked his body with constant pain, often making it impossible to get out of bed. This man told me personally that Dean had relieved the severity of his pain to the point that he could travel and lead a normal life, albeit the disease continued to dwell in his body.

People were now beginning to come to the Progress Agency to see Dean the spiritual teacher. He received invitations to speak at different venues. Some people asked to become his students. The Progress Agency was gaining a reputation but nobody, not even ourselves, could say for what.

The Progress Agency conference in Dhaka was scheduled for April 1992. The Earth Summit was to take place in June.

The time quickly rolled up on us. Dean had already left for Bangladesh. I was finishing some business and would trail him in a week. I would bring the camera man with me. His name was Greg Wendt. Greg was a quiet, quirky guy who had recently met an Ananda Marga monk and had begun to meditate. At the time, he worked for a New York City TV program and moonlighted by shooting advertising for Channel 35.

Greg had also begun doing volunteer work for the Progress Agency. When we invited him to come to Bangladesh, he readily accepted the offer. Our agreement was that we would cover all his camera expenses, room, and lodging, but that he had to pay his own plane fare.

On the flight over, I gave Greg more information about our spiritual heritage and tried to prepare him for what to expect. In this latter endeavor, it was the blind leading the blind. "Shoot everything that is not forbidden," I finally told him, and turned away to try and get some sleep.

The flight to Bangladesh was long and tedious, except for a brief layover in Abu Dabbi. If you ever want to see an exotic airport, check out Abu Dabbi. It is not big, but the architecture is very unique. The building has no corners or straight walls. In the center of the building rises a large funnel shaped column covered with small lime green tiles. It expands so that the mouth of the funnel turns into the ceiling above the second floor. The green tiles graduate into dark blue tiles that eventually cover the entire ceiling. The green "tree" grew in the center of a court having tables and chairs and surrounded by food stands and gift shops on the first floor. On the second floor, travelers sat on taffy colored leather chairs and waited for their flights. The chairs faced large curved windows that revealed the desert beyond. It stretched as far as the mind could see.

We reached Bangladesh just before dawn. As the big jet lumbered down to ten thousand feet, I strained my eyes to see below. I saw only a great blackness sprinkled sparsely with tiny points of light. As we continued to descend, I could make out small villages, foliage, and clumps of coconut trees. "Here we go . . . ."

By the time we touched down, the sun had come up—a nonintrusive pink-orange disk in a thick gray sky. There was something riveting about stepping off the plane onto the tarmac. It was the feel and smell of the air, an exotic mix of dew, smoke, garbage, feces, and trees. The air is also heavy, so you feel like you're in another dimension, the way you do when your head is under water.

A battered transport bus picks us up and takes us to the terminal. There are no seats on the bus. We all stand politely, packed in tight. Greg and I are the only white faces, but nobody seems to notice. I'm beginning to think that only white people are fixated on skin color.

Bangladesh is the most densely populated country on the planet with fifty million people walking around on a piece of real estate the size of Wisconsin. Things get real interesting during the monsoon season when half of this land gets submerged in water and people must take makeshift boats to get to where they're going.

As we waited for our bags, I was wondering why it didn't seem that crowded. I hadn't see the glass wall yet that separated the passengers from the throng of humanity.

We picked up our bags, went through customs, walked through the swinging doors and there was the wall of humanity that stretched from one end of the airport to the other, at least twenty people deep. Greg and I stood gawking at the glass wall trying to figure out our next move. We knew someone would meet us, but who would that be? How could we possibly connect? These were the days before cell phones. We pondered our situation for several minutes behind the security of the wall.

Suddenly I spotted Alam! He looked like a prince among paupers. He wore a long, pressed beige garment and the Muslim small round cap called a tufi. The cap was braided with gold. He had an entourage of four or five men behind him and they were muscling their way through the crowd, coming toward the wall. When he saw us, we waved and he signaled for us to go out the door in the center of the wall and meet him there.

Between Greg and I, we had seven or eight bags that contained clothing for a couple of weeks, gifts for Huzur and the orphan boys at Ibrahimpur, my sleeping bag, papers for our conference, etc. Greg had tons of camera equipment. We pushed our way through the doors and stood in the swarming mob. The smell of the day and the din of the crowd were mesmerizing. Immediately a man grabbed two of my bags and moved away quickly motioning for us to follow him. I jerked a bag back from him and demanded that he give me the other bag. He resisted, but relented and melted back into the crowd. Two other guys pushed their way toward us offering to take our bags. No . . . NO.

When Alam reached us, he smiled broadly and greeted us as the Sufis do with a nod and the right hand held over the heart. As'Salaamu Alaykum. Wa Alaykum Salaam.

Then quickly, with decisive moves, he ordered each man behind him to take our luggage. We did not stand on ceremony, but moved quickly in a tight line through the crowd toward the exit.

Outside a blast of hot, smelly air and blinding sunlight withered our senses. Deathly looking beggars reached out to touch us as we passed. A mother with a shrinking baby and an old man with no eyes absently moved their mouths at us as we passed. We did not dare to stop and give money unless a riot ensued. Even so, it always punished my sense of humanity to see such misery up close.

We hurried through the crowd and Alam barked at the cab and rickshaw drivers who relentlessly approached us. We reached a white van and the men threw our luggage in the back and we piled in. Greg was telling the men to be careful with the camera equipment. They didn't understand him.

Flags of the Dayera Sharif and the United Nations flew from the van. I guessed that this was because Alam had been chosen as a Peace Ambassador by the UN and had been involved in peace negotiations between Israel and Saudi Arabia at one time.

As soon as we started moving, the driver blew his horn incessantly and swerved around each pedestrian, rickshaw, motor bike, ox cart, and anything else that got in his way. People gave us dirty looks as we passed. Greg and I tightened our lips and raised our eyebrows at each other. We were obviously very important with our big shiny van and the flags waving and the people had better get out of our way.

As we reached downtown Dhaka, traffic got very dense. Bumper to bumper could not touch this. It was more like sardines in a can. At one point, we came upon panicked people elbowing their way in an attempt to get out of the crowd. Ahead we glimpsed tear gas clouds and police in riot gear. Our driver quickly made a detour. Alam turned to tell us that it was university students. They were always protesting something, he explained. I had an image of the children of the elite of Dhaka attending classes without text books, supplies, or computers, and having to pay a high tuition for the privilege.

I couldn't help but notice how different Alam was now. When I had seen him in New York, he was quiet and humble. Here his bearing commanded the attention one would give a ranking general. When he spoke those around him looked attentive, deferred to his words, bowed quickly, and moved quickly.

I recalled that Dean had told me about an incident where Alam had gotten very angry at him on his first trip. Alam had yelled at him and repeatedly stamped his feet because Dean had refused to make a visit with him to meet some political crony. I could see now how that might happen. In time, Alam would turn out to be the embodiment of evil, but that is a story for another day.

The van veered down a narrow, dirty street. I looked out the window at a small cluster of people standing around a jerry-rigged structure made of wooden crates, cardboard boxes, and blankets. It was the kind of thing my brothers and I would build in our basement when we were kids, but this was actually some people's home. Down the street such structures stretched to the horizon.

The van came to a stop in the middle of a street. Immediately, two large white metal doors swung open on our left and the van pulled inside a small compound. This was it—the Dayera Sharif headquarters in Dhaka. The compound was called Azimpur.

I took a long deep breath and looked at Greg. Okay then. The driver pulled open the side door on the van and we got out and looked around. Alam indicated that the building we were facing was the mosque (masjid). I nodded. As I looked around, I noticed we were in a small rectangular courtyard surrounded by buildings ranging from one to three stories in height. Alam led us through a small doorway away from the mosque and up a narrow, enclosed staircase. At the first landing I noticed a locked door. Alam opened the door and we walked inside with the men carrying our luggage.

I would be staying in this room with Dean. I could see his stuff piled about and mosquito netting over his bed. The room was large and bright with white curtains and pink walls. There was an old TV in the corner and bookcases and file cabinets. Alam told me that Huzur and Dean were in the mosque. I should unpack my things, wash up, and meet them down there.

He left with Greg and the others and I began to unpack. I hung the bag with my suit over a closet door and got my toiletries and walked into the bathroom. It had the usual Indian style toilet and plastic buckets. Oh, I remember this. There was, however, a sink with running water and a mirror over it . . . and a hook for a towel. I put my face up close to the mirror and studied it. I looked worried. I didn't think I would be.

I heard a knock on the door and when I walked out of the bathroom, Alam was in the room. He had a lungi and a tufi for me. "Here," he said "you will be more comfortable in this, I think."

I became aware of the heavy, sweaty blue jeans I was wearing and knew he was right. "Thanks," I said. Alam grinned shyly and left.

A lungi is a wide loop of cloth as long as your legs. You step into it and pull it up to your waist. Then you grab the loose material on each side, twist and tie the two ends together so that the material now fits tightly around your waist. I tried it on and then took a quick bath, shaved and put on my new clothes. The lungi Alam gave me was made of cotton and was light and cool. It would solve the problem of the hole-in-the-floor toilets. I put on a short-sleeved shirt, left it hanging out and put the tufi on my head. It was white with a decoration in copper-colored thread.

I was ready. I walked to the door of the room, but hesitated. I sat down on the floor and breathe deeply. "Dear God, thy will be done."

I remembered that I had brought gifts for Huzur and decided this would be the best time to give them to him. Dean had told me that there were not many amenities in Bangladesh and that people liked practical gifts.

I had brought Huzur a big bath towel, a bottle of shampoo, some nice soap, and several packages of flowers and vegetables seeds. I hoped these simple gifts would be okay. I didn't know what to give a spiritual master. When I had met Baba, I hadn't given him anything. I felt bad about that now, but I just hadn't thought about it at the time.

So Dean and my friends had told me that Huzur was a spiritual master. This filled me with over-sized expectations along with a healthy dose of skepticism. I just hoped Huzur was at least ... *real,* whatever that meant. I knew he couldn't measure up to Baba, but he needed to be ... something. I needed to be impressed. There was a lot riding on this, not the least of which was my business, my friendship with Dean, and my spiritual compass.

I left the room and walked down the hall tentatively with my small pile of gifts. I walked down the stairs, passed a room on the landing with people in it, and into the courtyard.

The mosque was a rectangular building that was attached at a right angle to the building that provided the residence for Huzur's family, which was also the building in which Dean and I were staying.

Thick, square, concrete pillars and a roof protected a walkway that stretched the length of the mosque's front wall. The wall itself had large openings so that people could see into it or even sit on its ledges. As I approached the mosque, I could see movement inside. I walked past the van that was still parked where we had left it. I continued through the thick square pillars and through the doorway into the mosque.

The mosque was a large room with nothing in it. The walls were painted in a soothing green and brown. The floor was smooth stone tile. Men in tufis sat along the walls or in small clusters around the room.

I looked around and saw Dean sitting off to the left in the small group of men. I walked up to them and sat down facing Dean and

A MATTER OF STYLE

Huzur. Dean grinned broadly at me and immediately introduced me to Huzur. A man in the group translated Dean's words and Huzur looked up at me.

I found myself looking into an old man's face that sent a distinct electric current through me. As strange as this sounds, it was kind of like seeing a beautiful woman. I felt exhilarated, almost giddy, confused. I looked closer into his face. Huzur was in his late seventies, somewhat stoop shouldered. He had dark skin and a wispy, white beard. He wore a white tufi and a light blue cape of some kind. As I sat there just inches from Huzur my sense of amazement continued to grow. Why was he affecting me this way? What exactly was I looking at here? Certainly, he could be a great wizard of some kind. The fact that he was a purported miracle-maker could be giving me the buzz I felt. But I felt intuitively it was more than this. Huzur tolerated my scrutiny with a quiet, trusting, almost shy demeanor.

"What's that, Chuck?" I heard Dean say.

I looked at him and saw him nodding at the gifts I had brought for Huzur.

Now it was my turn to be shy. I told him quietly that they were gifts for Huzur. A man immediately translated my words and Huzur perked up. He sat up straighter and inched a little closer to me like a kid might. This tickled me and immediately relaxed me. I began by giving Huzur the packets of flowers that were on the top of the pile. This immediately caused a great sensation. He pointed excitedly at the flowers on the packages and talked animatedly with the men in the group. Everybody smiled and looked happy. More men came around our little circle and added their comments.

Then I gave Huzur the vegetable seeds. Some he obviously recognized, like zucchinis, and nodded approvingly. Some he looked at and screwed up his face to make us laugh. He'd make a little comment in his crackly voice and everyone would laugh heartily.

This was great! I was comfortable now. More than comfortable, surprisingly I felt I was among family and old friends. I looked at the faces of the men around me. Their faces were sublime. I looked back at Huzur and another piece of the puzzle fit into place. He was a great wizard, for sure, but he was more than this. He was our grandfather! He was the grandfather that everybody wanted when they were growing up. He filled your heart with a contagious happiness. You had no choice but to love him. You got sucked into his funniness, his wisdom, his magic, and his twinkling eyes that melted your defenses. I could see his eyes twinkling with love for me, like I was visiting my ideal grandpa's place for summer vacation.

When I gave Huzur the bath towel, soap, and shampoo, I had tears in my eyes. He accepted them so graciously, as if they were the best gifts he had ever received because they came from me.

I looked intently at Huzur. He looked shyly back. Then, without looking away from me, he told a translator to tell me that I must be tired from my long journey. Perhaps I would like to meditate and rest. He said I could meditate in my room or in the mosque.

I wondered what the others thought of this last statement—a yogi meditating in their mosque. I looked around a little sheepishly, but to my surprise it didn't seem to faze anyone. They still looked happy as kids on a picnic.

I closed my eyes, took a deep breath and then stood up. I gave Huzur my namaskar and he placed his hand over his heart.

I honor the Divinity within you with all the divine charms of my mind and all the love and cordiality of my heart.

As'Salaamu Alaykum. May peace be upon you.

I decided to take another shower. In the shower stall, I poured bucket after bucket of water over my head, keeping my lips as tight as I could make them. I used soap and shampoo. The morning had been hot and sticky and the water was a wonderfully cool temperature and I didn't want to stop.

Greg knocked on the door while I was getting dressed. I told him that I was going to meditate in the room. He said he was going for a walk with the video camera to take some shots.

"Great, see you later."

I went to brush my teeth absently, but fear grabbed my guts. The water! I immediately got my Pur filter and filtered a liter of water to use to rinse my mouth out after brushing. I told myself that I needed to take my time and think through my actions here. "Don't space out," I reprimanded myself. "Sh*t."

I put a T-shirt on and the lungi that Alam had given me. I unrolled my sleeping bag on the floor and sat down feeling cool and comfortable. I was in a good mood.

I looked around the room and out the ornamental window grates to the rooftops and minarets of Dhaka. It was a foreign cityscape. The noises of the street, the smell of the air, the bleached-bone whiteness of the buildings . . . I knew the coming week would also be filled with work. I needed to make sure I didn't get sick. I reminded myself to filter more water before I left the room.

I closed my eyes and began to slow down my breathing. "Baba, may I serve you this day," I prayed as I did every day before starting to meditate. I went through a series of yogic practices to energize and focus my mind. I decided not to go down to the mosque, but to stay in my room and meditate. I could use the peace and quiet and time alone.

There is an old saying, "If you want to make God laugh, tell him your plans." My plans for peace and quiet must really have been hilarious for God because almost immediately after sitting to meditate, a brilliant, full-bodied image of Huzur appeared in my mind! It was totally unexpected and extraordinary. It was much more real and powerful than anything my imagination had ever conjured up. I opened my eyes to get my bearings, but was shocked to find Huzur standing the same way in the room. I looked closely.

It wasn't Huzur in flesh and blood. It was rather a glowing energy field of some kind, like a holograph but alive, in 3D, and full color. He looked at me and smiled playfully as if to say "Isn't this cool!?"

I closed my eyes. I opened my eyes. It didn't matter. He was standing there, looking at me....

My heart began to pound harder. Needless to say, I was awestruck. But soon, the feeling of awe and happiness turned into a nagging, troubled feeling. I remembered what Baba Anandamurti had said about great yogis and master magicians being able to project their ectoplasmic mind stuff outside their own bodies and create images that other people could actually see. I knew this was what Huzur must be doing and now I didn't like it.

If truth be told, from what I had experienced of Huzur down in the mosque, I felt that he was a spiritual master. Masters are different from normal men. The way they communicate is different. They can enter your mind and meld with it. It is extraordinarily personal. I felt that Huzur, like Baba, was someone I would do anything for— but the fact that he was doing this now, to me, when I was sitting down for my private time with Baba, bothered me. It disappointed me. He had gone too far.

Didn't he realize that I was the disciple of one of the greatest masters that ever walked the face of this earth? I had met and been touched by God Consciousness in a human body. Baba had altered my DNA. He had given me new spiritual information in great detail about how consciousness works and how it is able to transform itself and manifest in different forms. He had unraveled the ancient mystery of body, mind, and spirit for me. He had explained reality from every angle, explained life-and-death, animate and inanimate —he had revealed these things through demonstrations so that I could actually see the workings of which he spoke. He had given me the spiritual tools to reach my highest potential as a human being. Moreover, his knowledge had all been written down in the Ananda Marga books and continued to circulate in conversations between Margi and Margi as we met in passing from place to place around the planet. Baba trained us hard as spiritual warriors. He had poured himself into us so that no one could lead us astray or do us harm. He was the measure of myth and men for us. We were not easily tricked or impressed by the ego expressions of others, no matter how dazzlingly or lofty.

As I peered into Huzur's luminous being, I interpreted his action as a "stunt," almost a cheap trick to get my attention, to make me think how great he was. Why? So that I would become his disciple most likely. I felt a certain disgust and sadness arise in me. He had no idea who I was, or who Baba was. And yet there he remained, his eyes twinkling at me.

I closed my eyes to concentrate. It didn't help of course because Huzur remained in my mind as well, but somehow, I felt I could think better. Suddenly, it struck me. I knew how to solve this matter.

It came down to this. I wanted Huzur to understand that I was a faithful disciple of Baba Anandamurti. I was not for sale. I wanted to communicate this in a way that wouldn't hurt his feelings, even though his actions required me to point out the crudeness of his intent and the limits of his power.

I opened my eyes and spoke to him. "Huzur, please bring Baba here," I said quietly. I expected this would quickly short-circuit the situation.

The apparition of Huzur apparently heard me because he raised his eyebrows in surprise. He drew his right hand up to his side and opened his palm. Presto! There stood Baba Anandamurti!

Oh my God! Baba stood there in his familiar white garb smiling sweetly and giving me his namaskar (spiritual greeting). Baba and Huzur looked at each other and then back at me. Masters. the Masters. the Masters.

This blew my boat out of the water. I couldn't make sense of any of this except to know that it was miraculous. Yet, in my ignorance, stupidity, and hard-headedness my mind remained in denial. I closed my eyes again. They were both there. I opened my eyes again. They were both there. I rubbed my eyes. They were both there. They weren't doing anything. They weren't going anywhere. They were just looking at me. They both looked happy though, like it was Old Home Week or something and here we all were. How great!

Instead of short-circuiting the situation, my strategy had short-circuited my brain. I wished it would stop jerking around for just one damn second because another part of me knew that I was in the middle of a colossal miracle here and I was going to miss the whole thing if my brain kept freaking out. What I really wanted to do was to get down on my hands and knees and kiss their feet. I wanted to hold their legs so they couldn't get away. I wanted to cry and discharge all the hurt and pain of my life. I wanted all the bullshit out of my system so I could be free. I wanted to be free to love things. This experience was making me realize that I couldn't love things like I really wanted to. I could feel all my stupidity, fear, and baggage holding me back. I realized now what true freedom is—it's being able to love with nothing holding you back. No self-doubt, no fear, no anxiety, no suspicion or jealousy or envy. So much garbage was holding me back. My heart ached, my guts crunched in spasms.

Then my mind took off like a supercomputer—like you see in the movies with blue numbers flitting at the speed of light until it cracks the code.

And then it suddenly stopped. The code was cracked. I could see it written on the screen in my mind:

"God is existing perfectly in two separate bodies. Even though the bodies are different, God is existing perfectly in each."

And then came the ultimate realization:

"*God is existing perfectly in everything that is, all the time, everywhere.*" Something like sewer gas and gunk had been building up in my heart. Then the lid blew off like a manhole cover, flipping like a tiddlywink fifty feet in the air. Emotional crap just poured out of me. Hot tears flooded my face. I groaned and rocked back and forth. Sweet God, why are you so good to me. Why are you so good to me?

It all came out. I let it all go.

I don't know how long I remained lost in this catharsis, but when I looked up, surprisingly, Huzur and Baba were still there. They hadn't left me. Maybe it was because they didn't want me to doubt that this had really happened to me. When he saw me looking at him, Huzur put his hand over his heart and faded out. Baba remained a little longer. Then he gave his namaskar and followed Huzur back into the Nothingness.

I sat there for a long time, my insides the aftermath of a tornado. I had just experienced a God that is bigger than any name or form, bigger than any religion or spiritual master. That this God can exist in a human body and when He/She does, that body can express omnipotence, omniscience, and omnipresence. This God can exist in more than one of these bodies at the same time. I also learned that everything is an expression of God. Nothing has existence apart from God. Matter was not king after all. This was no longer a question of philosophy, conjecture, or blind faith. It was a fact of experience.

Slowly, I pulled myself together and walked down to the mosque. I didn't want to be alone anymore, but I still wanted to be by myself. When I walked into the mosque, I didn't engage anyone, but sat quietly against the back wall hidden in the shadows cast by the pillars blocking the light of the late afternoon sun. I folded my legs under me in the meditation pose and closed my eyes. I listened to the quiet murmur of the voices in the mosque and the muted cacophony that came from the streets outside the compound.

After a half hour or so I opened my eyes and looked around the room. I was beginning to enjoy its peacefulness and simplicity. It occurred to me that the men were observing the last days of Ramadan and were all fasting. I also realized that while I had not eaten for hours, I wasn't hungry. I remembered that I forgot to filter more water as I had wanted to do. I thought how quickly the mind returns to the mundane.

Suddenly, I found my eyes locked in contact with Huzur's. He was sitting as before with a small group of men, but now he was sitting at the other end of the mosque. As we looked at each other, he smiled and leaned over to speak to a man at his left. The man rose on one knee to see over the heads of the others in the circle and looked at me. He said "Huzur said to tell you that it's all just a matter of style."

I closed my eyes and tears welled up in me again. What had happened to me was not just in my imagination. It was real. I had been touched by God again. Huzur knew exactly what had transpired up there in my room. The message that I had learned, he now confirmed. The difference between Huzur and Baba was only a matter of style. Their underlying reality was the same. I looked around the mosque and I knew I was sitting in the house of God. And in this house, they called Divine Consciousness by the name of Allah.

Zikr

In the late afternoon, we took a ride around Dhaka, getting out of the van in the shopping district to walk around. We returned after sunset to have dinner in our room and hang out with Huzur's grandchildren—Sunni, Faiz, Mahmood, Anwar, Aynin, and Hariman. Dean played his guitar and entertained us all with his singing and funny antics. In the late evening we went back to the mosque for *Zikr*.

Zikr was a unique experience for me. About fifty men and boys sat on the floor in a large circle. Actually, we sat in an oblong formation that followed the rectangular shape of the mosque. Huzur held a large glass jar filled with one thousand brown beans, which he promptly dumped in a pile in front of him.

Zikr began with Huzur calling out a prayer, "Bismillah hir Rahman nir Rahim" (In the name of God, most merciful and most compassionate) and as he did so, he passed a bean to the man sitting on his right. Everyone answered in unison the same prayer. The same prayer was repeated rapidly over and over like a mantra and each time Huzur repeated the prayer, he would slide another bean to the man on his right, who would also slide a bean to the man on his right. In no time, beans were sliding from man to man all around the room. Because some men said the prayer faster than others, the recitation was not simultaneous. This created a sound like a continuous buzz. After some time, a new mantra would be chanted like "Alhamdulillah" (Praise be to God) or "Allah Hu Akbar" (God is Great). We continued saying the mantras until the last bean had made its way back to the jar in front of Huzur.

After about an hour of this, my butt was sore from sitting on the stone floor and my back ached from bending over to move the beans. My tongue felt large and pasty from racing to articulate the prayers. In short, I had had it. I leaned over and asked Dean how long this would continue. Dean looked at me with a little grin and told me it would go on through the night.

"Through the night!"

"Until 100,000 prayers have been recited," he whispered.

Okay, don't panic, I told myself. I looked across at four boys in a row. They were eight to ten years old. I saw that they were keeping up and told myself if they could do it, so could I. I hunkered down and concentrated on the prayers. I ignored my body's persistent complaining. After a few hundred more prayers, I didn't even notice Huzur passing beans anymore. I was keeping up with the group now. My eyes saw nothing of note; my ears heard only the buzz of the prayer. Even so, my mind wavered like a candle between the continual sound of prayer and the continual ache of my legs and back. It didn't matter anymore though, nothing mattered anymore, except for the doing . . . and the occasional points of stillness that occurred just inside the mind.

The praying did not go on all night but ended at about 4:00 a.m. When I arose to my feet, I wavered like a drunk. The ache in my back had gone away and I looked at things slowly and deliberately now. Reality had shifted more deeply into the back of my mind. The prayers reverberated in my subconscious. We went to sleep and woke up clear-eyed about 10:00 a.m.

In the afternoon, Alam took us to a "factory" where they made glass bracelets. Women in Bangladesh wear a dozen or more of these bracelets on each wrist as beautiful accessories to their long flowing saris.

The factory was a small cinderblock building with a single room. The room was about fifteen feet by twenty feet. No light entered the room except through the doorway. It took our eyes a little time to adjust.

When they did, we saw twelve women in saris squatting on the concrete floor in two rows facing each other. Between them ran a long copper tube that emitted a blue flame at each station. A pile of glass bracelets was set before each woman. Their job was to hold the bracelet to the flame so that the fire would seal the two ends of the bracelet and make them into complete circles.

The heat in the room was over one hundred degrees. As I watched the women, I thought about zikr the night before and wondered if the women's bodies ached in the same way that mine did. Could they think about Allah in this hellish sweatbox? The women did not look at us. They did not speak to each other. They did not smile. Only the owner, the one man in the factory, kept up a constant chatter with Alam. He brought out several boxes of bracelets and gave them to us. They were very beautiful. He wanted us to try and set up a business in New York when we returned. Alam said that it would help raise money for the Dayemi Complex.

Actually, I did take the bracelets to several costume jewelry wholesalers when I returned to Manhattan, but I was told that because they were made of glass, they could be dangerous. If one broke and cut someone, the seller could be sued. I wondered if the women in Bangladesh had this problem. In any case it was a deal breaker. The visit to the bracelet factory continued to have a haunting effect on me.

The Progress Agency Conference

The next two days were extremely busy. We had met Huzur's family, including all the kids and cousins, and had socialized as opportunities presented. Our main objective now was to prepare for our conference that would be upon us in a couple of days. Our goal was to bring attention to the upcoming Earth Summit and gain input from the organizations of Bangladesh to its proceedings.

Dean was right about Huzur's reach. We met with the leadership of Bangladesh's largest organizations. These included the Freedom Fighters who had battled Pakistan in their fight for liberation. Although the war had been over many years ago, the Freedom

Fighters had remained in existence to fight for the basic needs of its members. The leadership with whom we met claimed millions of members, but they were old now and didn't look like they could afford a decent meal. We couldn't gauge their true strength. In our meeting with them, they presented us with Freedom Fighter pins and made us honorary members. They were quiet, sincere, decent, very poor men. We liked them and they liked us and we all hoped that something good might come of our discussions.

We also met leaders of the farmers' union and the fishermen's union. We met high level government planners, and representatives from various mosques in Bangladesh, who, although not Sufis, were allies of Huzur. We met members of a Catholic organization that received funding from outside sources to run their projects. They had nice buildings and middle-class standards.

Huzur allowed us to invite monks and nuns of Ananda Marga to the conference. We later learned that he took a lot of flack for this. Ananda Marga had been sensationalized in the local papers as being a "Hindu" organization. In Bangladesh, this was the kiss of death because Hindus were considered to be the arch enemies of the Muslims. Huzur had been warned by his own people not to invite the Margis. Government agents from Central Intelligence had even come to lean on him not to allow Ananda Margis at the conference. Huzur stood his ground. While this splattered mud on the Dayera Sharif, it greatly enhanced the image of Ananda Marga. Up to this point, the Dadas, we discovered had been living in fear that they would be beaten or killed and their property destroyed.

While Ananda Marga was not a Hindu organization, to be painted as such stirred centuries-old animosities. These had been instigated and fomented by the English during their colonization of India. The English had always used the technique of "divide and conquer" to rule its subjects and in India; this meant dividing the Hindus from the Muslims, the two largest religions in the country. When England was finally forced to withdraw from India, the hatred between Hindus and Muslims foretold a bloodbath that would surely have led to civil war. Riots, lootings and killings had already broken out before the British had even withdrew. The political solution crafted by the British and accepted by Nehru, the first Prime Minister of India, was to create a separate state for the Muslim minority. While this solution sounded good in theory, creating a separate state in practice proved disastrous. The Muslims were concentrated in two areas of India, in the northeast and the northwest. While the Muslims were actually given a state called Pakistan, the state itself was divided into two entirely separate pieces of land that sat like two misshapen ears on the long face of India.

Bangladesh was originally called East Pakistan. The people of East Pakistan soon found themselves being mercilessly exploited by the more powerful West Pakistan where the seat of government was maintained. This led to a war between the two localities and it was in this war that East Pakistanis gained their liberation and in so doing, called their new nation Bangladesh.

With the exception of a notable garment industry, Bangladesh never had an industrial base. It was a nation of small villages populated by poor farmers and fishermen. This is still how things exist today outside of Dhaka, the capital.

The people that we met were mostly poor people. They had no business skills, nor technology. While we did meet educated people who had some skills, they had few resources with which to organize or mobilize.

The program agenda for our conference was typed on an old black typewriter with backup carbon copies. The program had to be typed several times so that we could have enough copies for the speakers and group coordinators to be able to gauge the flow of the day and the time of their sessions. The two hundred or so participants never received any handouts.

The conference was set in the courtyard of the Dayera Sharif which had been wonderfully transformed into a very inviting environment. A large white canopy covered the entire courtyard, shielding us from the sun and creating a feeling of unity and camaraderie.

A stage was also set up with a carpet on which the speakers sat. A podium stood in the center of the stage where each speaker could address the participants. Flags and other decorative items enhanced the setting and the people sat on folding chairs. I'll never forget the large plastic green buttons that were given to everyone. They had a hand-made spot of glue on the back that held a safety pin in place. On the front of the button around the parameter, it said "The Progress Agency Inc. (USA) Conference on Progressive Development". In the center it said, "In support of the UNCED Earth Summit, Brazil '92.'"

The place was packed by the time that Dean got up to welcome everyone and introduce the speakers. Huzur also welcomed everyone and lead us in a prayer that asked for Allah's guidance over the proceedings. The remaining speakers, who were composed of different religious leaders, including Ananda Marga monks, blessed the conference and reiterated the need for unity and planning.

Then it was my turn. I gave everyone an overview of the state of the world's economic and environmental condition and spoke about the alarm among nations that led the General Assembly of the United Nations to hold a series of global summits to address the deterioration of the Earth's life support systems.

I told everyone that the purpose of the Progress Agency conference was to discuss key issues related to the economy and environment of Bangladesh and to develop recommendations that we could take to the Earth Summit on their behalf. While it was certainly true that the national government of Bangladesh would be submitting its own analysis, we had learned from our experience at the United

Nations that the positions of people's organizations often differed from the official position.

When I finished speaking, we broke into small groups to begin discussions. We had previously chosen broad workshop topics —environmental issues, women's issues, political issues, cultural issues, health issues, agricultural issues, housing issues, etc.—and now the people voluntarily went to the areas that were assigned for each topic discussion. Our hope was to develop recommendations from each small group and return for a plenary session to gain consensus on a comprehensive report.

As the workshop discussions took place, Dean and I spent time with each group giving guidance on how to proceed. I went to the group that was discussing agricultural issues. Their position was that it was impossible to increase agricultural production in Bangladesh without land reform. They argued that the plots of the average farmer were so small that he could not increase production. I suggested that they try to think "outside the box." This was a phrase they had not heard before and because they rarely used boxes did not make much sense. I wasted a lot of time trying to explain what I meant.

What I meant to say was that we needed a positive recommendation. If land reform is an issue, what are the reforms that need to be made. How would these reforms be put into practice . . . . We need a recommendation that can elicit action. I only got more blank stares. Unruffled, I gave another example. If the plots of the farmers are too small, what if neighbors got together and formed a cooperative. Maybe they could collectively buy equipment that could save labor. Perhaps they could increase production at least by using the boundary land that separated the small farm plots. Maybe the farmers could diversify production and reach a larger market. Everyone nodded. This, they understood. They still wore serious faces though. I began to sense that our format for problem solving was either not familiar to them or maybe they thought it was a waste of time. I left them to think more about their own recommendations.

I next went to the group on women's issues. I found the women sitting passively listening to a man tell them what their problems were. I immediately became annoyed. I said that the women should be talking and the man should be listening. The women should be discussing the issues that make it difficult for them to perform their roles as women, as mothers, providers, as social beings. "That is just what I am telling," the man said.

"No," I said. You are telling them as a male authority figure what is the problem with them. The women know best what problems they face. They need to say what these problems are among themselves and recommend solutions that work for them.

"Do you understand?" I said, looking into the face of each woman trying to get them to nod in affirmation. Again, serious, impassive faces. One woman said in a quiet voice, "One problem is that the women are not listened to."

"I think that is a large problem," I said. "Why don't you talk about this for a while and see if there is some solution you can come up with. Okay? Can you do this?" I again looked at the women and they nodded yes. I looked at the man. "It will be your job to listen and not make any suggestions. Listen to what the women have to say. Can you do this?"

The man squirmed in his seat and looked frustrated. I asked him pointedly again. He said the women were not used to thinking in such a manner and needed guidance. I responded that given the opportunity they would begin to think in their own interest and once this happened it would be better for everyone. The man was not convinced.

I patted him on the shoulder and left to visit the other groups. In meeting with the other groups I could tell that the people did not easily think about taking matters into their own hands. They talked repeatedly of needing more supplies from the government, from outside governments, or NGOs like the Progress Agency.

"What can you do for us?" I was repeatedly asked. We can help you organize to help yourselves, I responded. Neither the value, nor the logic of this offering was readily appreciated. It does not come easy for an impoverished, poorly educated, and colonized people to think clearly and rationally about improving their condition by virtue of their own unity and internal resources. The reports from the working groups reflected the mindset that more resources and a better strategy were required from national leadership and from foreign interests. This was unquestionably true, yet it was the most debilitating mindset to have. Dependence upon outside forces that had their own agenda would continue to impoverish the people and yet it was impossible for the people to understand any other way.

Quite simply, they argued, when you don't have anything, how can you be expected to create positive changes. You have no tools to create change. While this seemed like an obvious truth, they did not see that transformation must begin with internal changes. The people needed first to change their own vision of themselves and what they are capable of achieving. They did not understand that once you empower yourself the tools will become more readily available.

When it came time to make reports to the plenary, the most interesting report came from the women's issues group. Immediately, the only man in the group rose and walked briskly to the podium. Dean and I looked at each other and rose immediately to our feet. I announced from the loud speaker that because this was a report on women's issues, we wanted to hear the report from a woman. The man would not be cowed by such nonsense and continued to walk determinedly to the stage. Dean walked toward him and stood in his path but the man would not stop. I left the podium to help Dean.

We literally had to block his path and get in his face with angry words to stop him. We asked again for a woman to give the report and the woman, who had spoken up when I visited the group, rose and went to the podium. She introduced herself in a quiet voice and said she was an attorney who was employed by the government. Geez. We wondered what relentless male chauvinism must look like to an intelligent woman of this caliber. She spoke hesitantly but eloquently about the condition of women in Bangladesh and said that women needed more opportunities in schools and jobs to meet their needs and fulfill themselves. It was a great statement and Dean and I both thanked her afterwards. She nodded impassively.

After all the reports were made, we ate a meal provided by the Dayera Sharif and talked informally about many things. People were wearing the big, green plastic buttons that Alam had made for conference attendees. We had collected all the statements from the groups and continued to discuss the possibility of an ongoing planning process. Dean and I were hopeful that we could somehow continue this process. While this never happened, we were able to synthesize the material from the groups and get it into the hands of the leaders of the People's Forum, who used it in putting together their documents at the end of the Summit.

It was a good day. By the time people had gone through the workshops, listened to reports, and eaten a good lunch, they were in a pleasant mood. Most people left feeling uplifted.

Dean and I felt like we had accomplished something. What that was we couldn't say. If nothing else, Greg had filmed the event and we knew we had some good footage to develop a promotional piece for the Progress Agency. More than this, we knew we had met key people from across many sectors of Bangladesh society and we could not help thinking that if we maintained a relationship with Huzur, we might have access to an entire country within which to promote and implement

Prout theory. When I went to my room to meditate, I could not shake the thought from my mind that the Progress Agency might actually be getting off the ground.

In the evening, Alam took Dean, Greg, and I to Rosie's parents' house for dinner. Rosie was Alam's second wife. The first was Huzur's daughter who lived in Dhaka with her children, three of whom were fathered by Alam. We found out that Huzur's family did not know about Alam's second marriage. In New York, Alam presented Rosie as his *assistant* at United Nations functions. Huzur would never have given permission for this second marriage. The issue remained hidden or at least not discussed by the family. As it stood, Dean and I both liked Rosie. We had met her on several occasions and in fact, Rosie had cooked the food for one of the Progress Agency forums at the UN. We felt it would be interesting to meet her parents and discover her roots. Rosie seemed out of place in New York culture. Her husband was her authority in all matters. He made all decisions for her and she dared not speak up to him. We did not know how much this could be attributed to Alam's dictatorial nature or the culture of Bangladesh and Islam.

I had never been in a private home in Bangladesh before and I wanted to see what one looked like. Rosie's parent's house was on a quiet street on the outskirts of the business district of Dhaka. The road was dusty and pockmarked. There were no lawns or trees the way we think of them in the States. There were, however, flowering bushes and a few small trees on the street. A high, black wrought iron fence ran around Rosie's parent's home that belied the sense of serenity the quiet street suggested. We parked the van on the street and Rosie's father came out to unlock the gate and greet us. He was about sixty years old and had a slight build. He wore white pants, a dhoti, and white tufi. He had silver hair and a white, closely cropped beard. He smiled at us gently and ushered us along with small movements of his hand.

Inside the house the rooms were simply furnished but comfortable. There was a couch with chairs in the living room. The walls were painted darker than the pastels that I was used to. We were immediately taken to the dining room and were asked to take our seats around the table that had already been set. We made small talk with Rosie's father, telling him how much we liked Rosie and he smiled appreciatively and shyly standing with his hands folded below his waist. While we talked, the cutest little girl, perhaps nine or ten years old, in a blue dress and barefooted, entered the room with an aluminum pitcher and began to fill our glasses with water.

I watched her glide around the table unobtrusively and thought she might be a servant, but her skin was more luminous than most children's I had seen in Bangladesh. Her large black eyes were not dulled by malnutrition either, but sparkled like those of a happy child who had been cared for.

When she poured the water into my glass, I said hello to her. She glanced quickly at me and smiled. I asked her name when she had finished pouring, but she only stood beside my chair and smiled at me. I realized immediately that she did not understand what I had said so I nodded at her and she continued with their chore.

I don't know why the little girl struck me so, but I began to think that if children are given decent food and shelter and adults who care for them, they can steal your heart no matter what race, what culture or part of the world they come from.

After some time, Rosie's mother entered the room and we were introduced, in turn, by Alam. She was a pleasantly plump woman with long black hair. She wore a pink sari and glasses with one of the lenses completely blacked out. Her front teeth were also darkened. Rosie's mother only spoke Bengali, so she stood there smiling and nodding at us as Alam commented on each of us.

She said she was pleased to meet us and that the food was ready to eat. Her voice was husky and wheezy. The couple excused themselves now, went into the kitchen and returned again and again with bowls of food. Once the table could contain no more bowls, Rosie's mom disappeared again into the kitchen, while her father remained with us to ensure that any empty plates were immediately filled again before anyone could say a word.

It was an unusual custom for me. The hosts never joined us during the meal. We could not even coax Rosie's father to sit with us for a moment. He declined with a small wave of his hand and an embarrassed look on his face. Occasionally, Rosie's mom would return to see how things were moving along and then disappear back into the kitchen.

We ate rice, fried okra, beans and tomatoes, chickpeas, fish, fried potatoes, unleavened bread, and drank pitchers of water. We ate pudding for dessert and drank coffee. Only after having one's plate filled at least three times and after formally and determinedly protesting against a fourth refill was it acceptable to not eat any more food.

After dinner we waddled into the living room. Now it was permitted for the hosts to sit with us. We talked more about Rosie and a little about our work in Bangladesh. We were also joined by Rosie's brother and two sisters who came to visit. They were all sweet people and were happy that we knew Rosie and spoke so affectionately about her.

Rosie's parents said they were thinking about coming to New York in the next year or so to see Rosie. We said they must certainly visit with us so that we might reciprocate for such a fine evening. Alam translated everything with a smile on his face. Alam was wearing a violet silk shirt and white pants and looked quite princely sitting on the couch. Behind him, on the wall, hung a large tapestry of the Hajj.

I inquired about the little girl and Rosie's mom immediately called her into the room. Her name was Fatima. We were told that her mother had died and that Rosie's parents had adopted her two years ago. How fortunate she was, I thought. I made a fuss over her, telling her what a big help she was, how pretty she was, etc. Alam translated and she stood before me smiling her radiant smile filled with amusement and embarrassment that a strange man from America would be paying attention to her. Rosie's parents smiled proudly.

We left after some time, everyone in good spirits. We could now tell Rosie how sweet her parents were.

A Whirlwind Tour with Huzur

We would spend the next few days on a whirlwind tour of three rural compounds of the Dayera Sharif that would take us the length of Bangladesh and reveal more about the person we now called Baba Dayemullah.

The morning began with a meeting in Alam's office. He had the largest room in the compound. It consisted of a large desk at one end of the room and enough chairs for thirty men set tightly side-by-side along the other three walls. Pictures of Alam with UN dignitaries and imams, plaques, and certificates hung everywhere. Flagpoles with the flags of the Dayera Sharif and the UN stood on each side of his desk. This was Alam's center of operations.

A disagreement between Dean and Alam as to our exact itinerary had begun. Alam, who had scheduled the tour, wanted us to stop in the village of a man named Abdul Aziz who had participated in our conference. The visit would take us off course and require additional hours of travel time. Dean apparently knew the man from a previous visit and considered him a self-serving opportunist. Dean's interpretation was that Abdul just wanted us to visit his village to bolster his status with his wives and with the villagers. He was flat set against going to visit him. "I'm not traveling twelve hours to see this man," he said resolutely.

Alam had other motives, which we could not decipher, but he was just as firmly committed to going to see Mr. Aziz. Things were beginning to heat up when a messenger came and told us that Huzur wanted to see all of us in the mosque.

We left Alam's office and found Huzur sitting on the floor in the mosque fingering his prayer beads. When we arrived, he put the beads in his pocket. He looked at each of us in turn. Then he held up his hands and began to count his fingers. One, two, three . . . up to twelve. He widened his eyes. He nodded at us to see if we understood. Then he shook his head, "no." Dean and I exchanged glances. Apparently Huzur was aware of the disagreement that was taking place in Alam's office and had called us to the mosque to weigh in on the discussion. Well, that settled it. We would not be going to Abdul's village. Alam said nothing, but turned and walked away. Dean, Huzur, and I smiled at each other. Later, when we were back in New York, we received a photo from Abdul Aziz sitting by himself under a banner that said Welcome Progress Agency. A nice dig.

We packed up. Then Huzur, Dean, Greg, Alam, a driver, two disciples, and three kids, and I loaded into the van and headed out of Dhaka into the Bangladesh countryside. Huzur and Alam sat up front with the driver. Dean, Greg, and I sat in the middle seat and the other men and kids sat in the back.

Our first stop would be Ibrahimpur, Huzur's favorite retreat from Dhaka. We had been driving for hours on a narrow, two-lane paved road. The road was badly pitted and potholed so the driver would careen from side to side in a random jerky motion that made sleep or reading impossible. We drove on in the heat of day staring at the monotonous landscape. The scenery lacked any trees or vegetation to speak of. Flat, green fields ran on in both directions to the horizon. Occasionally, a small clump of trees or a cluster of huts too far from the road to make out any details would appear and then quickly disappear without making an impression. What was unusual, however, was the number of people we saw everywhere. I don't think there was ever a time during our entire journey that we did not see people moving about.

People on the roads. People in the fields. People gathered around road stands. Specs of people walking around distant huts. It was a little disconcerting to be in a rural area and see so many people.

For quite some time, Alam talked incessantly in Bengali into Huzur's ear. Huzur sat motionless facing straight ahead. Then Alam too became quiet and we drove on for a couple of hours dazed by the monotonous landscape and the dull roar of the hot wind rushing through the half open windows.

At one point, Huzur turned to Alam and said something. Alam nodded. About ten minutes later Huzur said something again to Alam. Alam did not respond. I did not think anything about it, but I noticed that Dean watched this interaction intently. I nudged him to find out what was going on. He told me that Huzur had requested to stop for prayer, but that Alam wasn't acknowledging him. According to Islamic law, a Muslim must pray five times a day. The times of prayers were set according to the movement of the sun. There was only so much time to pray in any given period. Alam's behavior was inexcusable. We were shocked that he ignored Huzur.

We drove on. Soon we came to a large village. The streets were lined with beat-to-sh*t wooden stands, each selling a couple of items. The food stands were particularly disgusting having greasy black wooden planks in front of their doorways, garbage on the ground and paint peeled, dirty window frames. The walls of the huts were raw, weathered wood, chewed up, and ratty looking at the bottom because of the water that soaked them in the rainy season.

As we rode through the town, I found myself looking for a place where we might get out and pray. Toward the end of the town we heard a loud bang and the van swerved off the road. The driver got out to inspect the situation and informed us that we had a flat tire. Everyone had to get out of the van. Fortunately, *as luck would have it,* we found ourselves on a large hill beside a green field with a gas station across the road.

Blankets were brought out and placed on the grass under a large tree. To see such a tree was remarkable in itself. We prayed with Huzur while the driver and Alam dealt with the tire. The Sufis did Salat and I meditated. The air felt refreshingly cool in the shade of the tree, yet it was difficult to concentrate on my mantra thinking about this turn of events.

When prayers were finished, we sat in a small circle. Huzur had a grin on his face that charmed us. How fortunate that we had been given the opportunity to say our prayers. We sat on the hill on a sunny day, enjoying the breeze, and watching two cows walk into a farm pond up to their chests. Bushes grew around the pond with little yellow flowers. The kids were laughing and enjoying themselves. Alam and the driver stood waiting in the filthy gas station.

After another hour of traveling, we came to another village. The town was a shoulder to shoulder collection of weather-beaten wooden huts and stands. We turned down a narrow, dirt road thick with people. The van barely made it around the corner and people had to stand flat against the buildings as we inched slowly down the road. It's possible that we were riding in the only vehicle that ever drove down this road. The people's eyes registered surprise as the sea would part and they'd find themselves a couple of feet in front of the van. At the same time, they seemed familiar with the van and many would bow and put their hands over their hearts in the Sufi tradition of greeting. Young men hung on the doors or stuck their heads in the window to look inside or say something. I knew that eighty percent of humanity could probably relate to the people of this village—overcrowding, few resources, no amenities, barely surviving. The people's faces were as weather-beaten as the old boards that made up their dwellings. Their eyes were dull and their teeth were broken and yellow. I didn't feel threatened, but I didn't want to get out of the van either. An image of Flash Gordon's clay people came into my mind and would not go away.

At another intersection, the van stopped. There was a discussion between Alam and the driver. The driver couldn't decide if this was the place to turn. I could see how it might be difficult to decide. There were no street signs. There were no signs period. Every shack looked the same and in fact you could hardly see the shacks for the multitude of people swirling in cross currents around the van. Eventually the decision was made to turn. We drove past more shacks and an endless stream of people before we came out again into the countryside. After about five minutes, we came to a small clump of stands and we turned between them down another dirt road. We came to a blue wooden arch that stretched over the road. The arch was ornately carved and said "Ibrahimpur." We could see a grove of trees ahead to our left and a long, two-story, cinder block building on the right with a fish pond in front of it. As we drove up to the building another building under construction came into view on the right. This was to be Dean's house, I was told.

Now we could see children, boys about eight to twelve years old, standing up ahead in what appeared to be the center of the compound. More boys joined them and a few adults. By the time we reached them, there were about forty or so people to greet us.

The driver pulled over and stopped in front of a concrete building painted blue. We got out slowly from the van and the boys eyed us curiously. These were the orphans that lived and went to school at Ibrahimpur. The blue building was the mosque. It set directly across from and at one end of the long, two-story building that served as the dormitory and school.

We followed Huzur into the mosque for prayer. Afterword we sat for a while, talked, and got our bearings. It was mid-afternoon. We would stay overnight and head south tomorrow.

I looked at the boys who were sitting with us. They wore checker-patterned lungis and tee-shirts, either blue or white. They all wore tufis on their heads. The boys looked healthy and their brown faces had a glow to them. I liked their vibration. They were not wild or chatty like the kids I was more familiar with. They were actually quiet and respectful. When they exchanged words or glances or laughed with each other, there was a sweet innocence about them.

When we walked out back into the sunlight, I could see the dimensions of the compound. With the mosque at our back, Dean's future house was to the right. There was also a little shack with a flour grinder in it. Before us was the two-story cinderblock building that stretched most of the length of the compound, but was only as deep as a room. The second story had a walkway with a metal banister and steps that went up to it on both ends of the building. Wooden doors, evenly spaced along the wall, opened into single rooms that served as classrooms and sleeping quarters. The boy's beds were made of roughhewn wood. There were no mattresses on the beds.

Huzur had a room on the ground floor across from the mosque. It too was simply furnished. One of the teachers showed Dean, me, and Greg to our room on the second floor. It was quite large and except for a couple of wooden platforms for sleeping, completely empty. The window frames had wrought iron grates that allowed us to look down on the fish ponds and the rice fields we had passed while driving up

We staked out our "cots" and rolled out our sleeping bags, then threw our gear underneath. It took us a while to figure out how to tie up our mosquito nets. The ceilings were ten feet high and we had to search for a ladder, some additional twine and nails to get everything hooked up. I can't say how the boys slept without mosquito nets, but I knew that without them we would have had a nasty night.

Greg was concerned about leaving his equipment in a room without a lock. Dean assured us that we need not worry about having anything stolen. Greg fidgeted. He had thousands of dollars wrapped up in his equipment and, with all due respect, Dean's simple assurance didn't cut it. I was a little nervous myself. It only took one person.

Dean walked over and sat down on Greg's cot. He told us a story about how someone had stolen his watch from his room while he was touring on his last trip to Bangladesh. He searched his belongings several times and thought back on his day to determine if he could have left it anywhere before he knew for certain that it was stolen. Not wanting to make a scene, but not wanting to let the event go unnoticed either, he finally reported the incident to Huzur. Huzur frowned seriously and immediately put the word out that the watch had to be returned immediately or else there would be dire consequences for the thief. The thief did not come forward. In fact, there wasn't a word from anyone about the watch for the rest of the day. Dean wrote the watch off and went to sleep.

The next morning a frightened man showed up early at Dean's room and confessed to stealing the watch. He humbly and nervously gave it back to Dean and begged his forgiveness. Dean thanked him for his honesty. Dean later found out, that during the night, the man had begun to bleed profusely from his mouth and anus at the same time. The bleeding did not stop until he went to return the watch.

Greg and I looked at each other. Yep, that was good enough for us.

In the evening, we distributed the toys that we had brought for the boys. They were simple toys like yoyos, balls and paddles, and balsa wood airplanes, but for the kids who had no toys at all, they were wonderful. It made me wish I had brought a volleyball or soccer ball.

The next morning after splashing water on ourselves from a bowl and doing our prayers, two boys brought a breakfast of rice and spicy vegetables on metal plates. We also had hot tea. Afterwards, Dean and I went for a walk around the compound.

We walked down the stairs at the far end of the building. After a few steps we were near a small brick hut that served as the kitchen. There were no stainless steel sinks in this kitchen, or wooden cutting boards; there wasn't any electricity or even hooks on the walls to hang pots. The "kitchen" was basically a dirt floor, lit by the sunlight that came in through the doorway. The floor was hard-packed and black from being saturated with cooking oil and human traffic. A pile of branches for making a fire sat along one wall. In the middle of the small room, an old women squatted. She held vegetables over an open pot and cut them in the air with a knife. It was dark in the room and I had to squint to adjust my eyes before I could see her. She barely looked at us, but continued squatting and cutting the vegetables. I guessed the dishes weren't washed in hot, soapy water or rinsed in bleach either.

Neither Dean nor I felt like hanging out in the kitchen this morning, so we said goodbye to the cook and stepped back outside. A couple of scrawny cows stood in a pen next to the kitchen. We knew what their destiny was.

Outside the kitchen a dirt path led away from the dormitory and classroom building. It was lined with trees with a fish pond on the right. It looked inviting so we took it. Dean and I were interested in sharing Baba Anandamurti's ideas about *Master Units* with Huzur and the custodians of Ibrahimpur. We talked excitedly about the possibilities.

A Master Unit, according to Baba, served as a hub for rural revitalization, which was a key tenant of Prout theory. It is a land-based economic unit that is self-sufficient in its ability to meet basic needs for its members. These include food, shelter, clothing, health care, and education. A Master Unit is also responsible for providing services to its neighbors including free seeds, education, and health care if necessary. Baba Anandamurti had started several such Master Units in India and had given the direction that Master Units should be created all around the world. In the United States, for example, there were several Master Units in different stages of development.

As we walked along the shaded path that looped around the pond, we met Huzur Baba. He was walking along an intersecting path that led to a field newly planted with banana and coconut trees. Baba smiled at us as he busied himself pulling dead leaves from some of the newly planted trees. The trees were about waist high and the interpreter told us that Baba had planted all the trees himself. Baba asked us if we liked what we saw. Actually, it was hard to keep up with him as he moved from tree to tree, pointing here and there to other plants and across to the fishponds and told us what he had planned for the land. Dean and I were both hypnotized by Baba's agility. He popped around more like a wood sprite then a man nearing eighty years old. As we watched Baba dart from plant to plant, the realization dawned on us at the same time that while we could discuss Master Units from a theoretical perspective, Baba was actually showing us one in operation! And he was making it happen with his own hands!

It should have been humiliating to us, considering how highly we thought of ourselves for the knowledge we possessed. Yet Baba's twinkling eyes and his joy at sharing his work with us made us feel included in the joy of it. "Do you boys like what you see?!" he asked. Baba Dayamullah had once told Dean that Baba Anandamurti was the master of all sciences. I never understood how he knew this because he had never met Baba or read anything about him, but as we had come to realize it took one to know one.

In the evening, one of the teachers told us that the boys and girls from the surrounding villages, as well as the boys in the orphanage, attend school at Ibrahimpur. There was no orphanage for the girls. Dean told the teacher that he looked forward to the day when the girls would have equal opportunities with the boys. The teacher, a young man in his twenties, bowed sincerely at Dean's words.

We enjoyed watching the orphan boys come and go. Their faces were wholesome, friendly, and curious. They had a nice, playful manner with each other and an easy laughter. It was also inspiring to see their devotion when we prayed in the mosque. I was secretly glad that US culture had not yet reached them. The boys had each other and they understood themselves by their relationships instead of by what toys they possessed or what they saw on TV or in the stores.

Amirabad was our next stop. It was a longer ride than the one we took to get to Ibrahimpur, and on the same kind of narrow pockmarked highway, with the occasional tank traps that caused the driver to swerve sharply when one appeared. Again, we watched the endless fields of rice and the occasional stretches of roadside shacks with glazed eyes.

An interesting diversion was a ferry boat ride across a slow-moving muddy river. The ferry had a loud clacking engine that belched black smoke. Several people, some with bicycles and a few with animals, crossed the river along with our van. The ferry had a little stand that sold Coke's and strange snacks. Interestingly, there was a small, weather-beaten prayer room on the ferry that could hold four or five people. We took turns praying and then came out and leaned against the rail to watch the distant shore approach.

A couple of small, one-story industrial buildings and a few shacks dotted the area around the landing and then we were back in the countryside again. I will never forget seeing so many people as we drove the endless miles of country road.

About 11:00 p.m., we reached what I thought was Amirabad. The night was pitch black and hung on you like a wet blanket. There was neither moon nor stars. It looked like nobody knew we were coming. Our arrival caught everyone off guard. Upon seeing us someone immediately put down a blanket for Huzur to sit on. Dean and I sat on a small bench under a small tree and waited. The place seemed uncharacteristically tense. When we looked back at Huzur, we discovered that he had disappeared into the night. Dean and I couldn't figure out what was going on. He told me, however, that this wasn't Amirabad. It was Satbaria and that Huzur had ordered Alam to stop here even though it wasn't on our itinerary. Dean was finely tuned to any exchange between Huzur and Alam, but I was not. More or less, I was just along for the ride and depended upon Dean to keep me appraised of our circumstances.

As we waited, a long column of men began appearing out of the darkness on a dirt path that ran past the buildings and the bench on which we sat. We could see them by the light of torches that some men carried. The men were villagers, small and slightly built, dressed in lungis and T-shirts, barefooted, sweaty, and caked with mud. They carried spades and shovels and plastic buckets. A steady flow walked by us, long faced, exhausted, perhaps as many as fifty men.

We found out later that Huzur had quickly called together some men to bring torches and they had walked together behind the school building. He had ordered them to point their torches in what revealed itself to be a half acre muddy hole about ten feet deep. Standing in the hole were men bare-chested with lungis pulled up short. When Baba saw the men, he was furious and ordered them out of the hole. The men touched his feet as they crawled out. Baba came back and sat on his blanket. The atmosphere was charged. Cooks were hurrying to prepare food for dinner. Soon a small group of local political representatives came over and knelt before Huzur. Huzur immediately told them if they were doing anything wrong, he promised them that Allah would punish them.

He got up and we walked with him through a small courtyard and sat in a room waiting for dinner.

One of the representatives returned and begged Baba's forgiveness. Apparently, while fraudulently using Baba's name, he convinced the government to give him money to build a fish pond. This man was working the villagers around the clock at half wage and pocketing half the money. The inhumanity of this act was reflected in the exhausted faces of the men. Digging a half acre pond with shovels and five gallon buckets was hard enough, without having to work sixteen hours into the blackness of night when the air was dead and the mosquitoes were on the hunt.

I never knew if Alam had authorized this act, but certainly Huzur's surprise visit and severe words must have fallen on more than one government representative. Once all of the men were freed from the pit and we had eaten, we left Satbaria.

Amirabad was similar to Ibrahimpur in its programs. It too had an orphanage, school, and farm. The compound was older than Ibrahimpur, however. The buildings were better made and possessed ornate, pale blue doorways and tile floors.

When we reached Amirabad, it was still night time. We were ushered to a long narrow room for our second dinner. Tablecloths were spread end-to-end on the floor and twenty or so men sat around talking softly and eating while other men in white shirts kept bringing in food and taking out empty bowls. Huzur was telling us that Sufis sat on their haunches when they prayed, just like dogs sit at their masters table waiting to be thrown a scrap of food. Everyone laughed at the analogy. I was a little put off by being compared to an animal, but I was attracted to how comfortable these people were hearing such a thing. My ego was too big. Huzur would tell us at another time that everything he did was Allah coming through him. His only work, he said, was to bow his head and say thy will be done. He called himself a slave of God.

As we ate, I noticed that everyone was eating with their fingers although they had given Dean, Greg, and me spoons with which to eat. As I watched them scooping rice and meat into their mouths with their fingers, Huzur must have read my mind. He had someone tell me that eating with one's hands was civilized. It made me smile. And as I considered the caliber of men in the room, I had no reason to challenge his statement.

The week in Bangladesh passed quickly—a sea of Brown faces, cinderblocks, and rice fields. Abject poverty is never easy to abide. It turns the stomach and wrenches the heart to see people clothed only in ratty T-shirts or worn cotton saris, too poor to wear shoes. The villagers lived in a place where every patch of earth that wasn't farmed was pounded into a filthy, worn dirt. Yet, somehow, the presence of Baba anesthetized the senses and kept the heart soft.

The people around Baba were poor, but their poverty was not abject or merciless. Their faces glowed when we were introduced to them. There was something extraordinary about their lives that could not be calculated in dollars or material wealth. Of course, there were people who circulated around Baba for the opportunities that he presented and would attempt to ingratiate themselves to us thinking we could further their careers or business interests. The devotees, however, wanted nothing from us. Rather, they were happy that we had come to see Huzur. It did not matter to them how many shared his grace, there was never any less to go around.

Do you know what its worth to be filled with boundless grace and magic? Would you pay money to know that at any moment something, some small event in your routine life, could open up and you would see the face of God? How much would you pay to feel a river of joy rush into you and wash away the fear, the brutality, the drudgery and the alienation of life and leave you solid and happy in your core? Would it be worth your while to know beyond a shadow of a doubt that you are the child of the Divine and are constantly being cared for? Would it be worth it to know these things, not through blind faith, nor someone telling it to you, nor by reading books, but through your own experience? Now, suppose that you would have the time and wherewithal to explore this deeper reality because society had created a political economy in which local people cooperated to meet their basic needs in a sustainable manner and you never had to worry about your survival. This is what Prout is about. Creating such a system. The gifts of the Masters are there for the taking if you are willing to take a chance.

Good Night

After Amirabad we returned to Dhaka. In the next afternoon, we went to the market in Dhaka to buy some gifts for our return. In the evening, we hung out in our room and ate dinner. The kids were with us and Dean was playing his guitar. We were joking with them and telling them about our families back home. Greg had his video camera running. After some time, Huzur called Dean, Greg, and me to his room.

Baba had a small room down the hall from ours. His bed took up most of the space so we either stood or sat on the side of the bed. Baba sat cross-legged at the head of the bed. He was not wearing his tufi so his long gray hair fell down to his shoulders. The meeting was informal and personal. He had called us to say goodbye. Baba said goodbye with gifts just as we had said hello. He gave each of us gifts in turn.

Baba gave me a wall hanging inscribed with the Suratu-l-Fatiha, the first chapter of the Koran and the prayer that millions of Muslims repeat each day as they perform Salat. I thanked him gratefully and told him that the next time that we met, I will have memorized the prayer. He smiled softly. He also gave me two beautiful pieces of cloth and a small bottle of medicine that smelled like licorice and mint. Surprisingly, over the course of the next year I used Baba's medicine to cure sore throats, remove splinters, and stop muscle aches. I don't know what else I could have used it for if I hadn't run out of it.

Finally, Baba gave me a prayer rug and a copy of the Koran. The Koran was completely in Arabic. Alam, who was in the room with us, whispered to me that this Koran was one that he himself had received as a gift from an Arabian Prince. Whether this was true or not I cannot say, but it seemed unlikely. In any case, the fact that Baba had given it to me was more moving than if I had received it from a prince.

What interested me more was a story that Dean told me about the prayer rug that Baba had given me. The Sufi prayer rug, he said, was the basis for the Middle Eastern myth about Aladdin and the flying carpet. Due to countless hours of prayer and meditation, Sufi masters were able to transport themselves to different levels of consciousness and even different physical locations. The common people did not realize the true cause of these mystical powers and attributed them to their prayer rugs which they called "flying carpets" or "magic carpets." Aladdin, the one who possessed the magic carpet, is actually Allah Din, which means the "Way of Allah." It was interesting to know that the myth of Aladdin came from Sufi tradition.

After I received my gifts, Baba gave me his blessing. I stood before him and he said a prayer. Then he took my head in his hands and drew me towards him. He blew on the top of my head. Then he looked me in the eye with his characteristic twinkle.

I watched Huzur give gifts to Greg and bless him in the same way and then we left. Alam left with us. Only Dean remained with Huzur.

It was now about eleven o'clock and I was tired. I looked at Greg thinking he might want to hang out some more but he wasn't looking too good. He said that he wasn't feeling well. I could see sweat on his forehead and touched his head. He was hot. I told him he better get some sleep. We would have to get up early to drive to the airport.

I organized my bags one last time and went to bed thinking about Greg. This was worrisome. Having a fever in Bangladesh could mean a lot of things, and none of them were good.

An hour or so passed before I was awakened from a deep sleep by a loud noise in the room.

"Dean... Is that you?"

"Yeah."

"What's happening?"

"I don't know."

"You don't know? What do you mean you don't know? Did you fall?"

There was another loud noise. This time I knew that it was Dean crashing into the coffee table in the middle of the room.

I rummaged out of my mosquito netting and turned on the table lamp by the head of the bed.

I shaded my eyes and squinted at Dean. I was groggy, but this situation didn't make sense to me. Dean and I could find that table blindfolded. We had eaten three meals a day off of it. The thing never moved. Something else was going on.

Dean looked distracted. He couldn't figure out what he was doing.

"What's up partner, are you feeling okay?"

"Yeah . . . Yeah," Dean said absently, continuing to walk around taking two or three steps in different directions.

"Dean. What. Is. Happening?" I asked emphatically.

"Huzur did something to me, Chuck."

Oh boy... This made the hair on the back of my neck stand up.

"What did he do?"

After a long pause in which we just stared at each other, Dean said "Huzur transferred his powers into me."

I felt the shock of adrenaline. My brain kept repeating "transferred his powers into Dean, transferred his powers into Dean?" Then the computer rebooted itself and the questions began.

How does somebody do that? What powers is he talking about? Can Dean do miracles now?

And then the bomb question came— is Dean God? Did my friend just become God realized?

I was frozen to the bed, staring at Dean. He continued to mill around the room.

I asked Dean to sit down beside me. I looked intently into his eyes. It looked like a hurricane had blown through him.

It didn't seem like this was a good time to begin asking questions. Even so, I couldn't resist asking Dean what he meant by Huzur transferred his powers into him.

Dean put his head down and replied "He said that I should bow my head and Allah will do his will through me."

I felt like jumping out of my skin. I kept staring into his eyes looking for . . . I don't know what. I couldn't stand this.

I wanted to ask him if he was God.... But I couldn't bring myself to do it. If he said yes, I wouldn't believe him. If he said no, I wouldn't believe him. I couldn't believe anything!

Something profound was happening again right before my eyes and all I could do was witness it. A part of me was in denial and accepted Dean's words as if they were just good news—like if I heard the Yankees won the pennant or that Dean just told me he inherited one million dollars. Yet at another level, I knew the consequences of what he was telling me would change my life forever. Nothing would be the same again. I watched Dean stare at the floor, occasionally looking up at me with a little smile. After several minutes we agreed we should get some sleep because we had to get up early the next day.

Even during the most profound experiences of our lives we are only witness to events. And yet we continue to believe that our lives are under our own control. We believe this at some deep level so that we do not even question the assumption.

It seemed like I had just fallen asleep when we were awakened by a knock at the door. Dean sprung up and went into the bathroom. I got up, put on my pants and turned on the light. It was still pitch-black outside and I could hear the patter of rain on the street.

There was another knock on the door and Alam walked in looking bright and cheerful. He was just checking to see if we were awake and getting ready.

I told him to check on Greg. He said he would and left.

Dean came out of the bathroom looking refreshed and in good spirits. I didn't see any of the dazed look on his face that I had seen just a few hours ago.

He wore a beige dhoti and tufi. His long black hair touched his shoulders. I watched him move around the room getting things packed.

Something was different—a little something that I couldn't quite put my finger on. Maybe it was the way he moved. Maybe his moves had more . . . intention. I didn't know how to explain it.

When I came out of the bathroom Alam, Greg, and two of the boys were in the room. Greg was definitely not looking good. He was complaining about feeling ill. We stood around him and stared. This was not good. Having a high fever in Bangladesh could be a matter of life or death. We could see the sweat on his face and his shirt was soaking wet. Dean and I exchanged glances. We could not stay here. We had to make the flight and we couldn't leave Greg behind. We would have to take our chances. Dean squatted down in front of Greg who was sitting on the bed and told him that our best option was to get back to New York as planned. Greg agreed. Dean patted his knee and told him he'd be okay.

We loaded up the van in the light drizzle and headed toward the airport. The darkness and dismal weather made things seem worse and Greg started to moan.

Dean sat next to Greg and put his arm around him. He comforted him and Greg became quiet.

I stared ahead through the bleary windshield as random images of Bangladesh came in and out of focus. I felt numb. I missed Huzur already.

After a few miles, Greg started talking about the great footage he had taken and how he couldn't wait to get back and put something together.

I was encouraged to hear him so enthusiastic. When we reached the airport terminal, the van pulled over and the driver turned on the inside light. Okay, this was it. Passports, airport tax, customs, baggage check. Time to focus. We were going back into the "real" world.

Alam got out and pulled the sliding door open. I turned to look at Greg and Dean. What I saw amazed me. Greg no longer looked sick. He wasn't sweating, his shirt was dry and he was acting quite normal. He was giving instructions that no one should carry off his equipment cases without him checking them first.

I couldn't believe the transformation. I then looked at Dean. Dean's face was soaked in sweat. His shirt stuck to his body. He looked back at me, but didn't say anything. He got out of the van and started carrying his bags into the airport.

As we went through our series of tasks and boarded the plane, it became increasingly clear to me that Dean had taken Greg's illness upon himself. What's more, Greg didn't seem to realize what had happened. He was his old self, talking away, apparently oblivious to the miracle that had transformed him.

I sat next to Dean on the plane. The signs of illness disappeared from him. I found myself thinking about him and images appeared to me of events over the last week. I saw him laughing with the children, their faces filled with happiness. I saw him touching the heads of the devotees that came to touch his feet. I remembered the visits he made to the sick family members in the villages. I saw him doing Salat in the mosque.

A profound sense came over me that my brother had become a christened one. We may still see through the same eyes, but no longer from the same depth of consciousness.

Suddenly, as I sat there looking at him, I was filled with a sense of awe and wonder. When he turned to look at me now his eyes were soft and filled with love. I swallowed hard and uttered a simple statement from my heart. I told him that I would be there for him. I didn't realize that this simple sentence would lead me to the greatest spiritual test of my life. Nor can I even say at this late date that I even knew what that simple sentence meant. Sometimes you don't understand things until a certain moment in time when everything properly aligns and it all becomes clear to you. It might be the littlest thing. It might signal your destiny. You don't know.

Dean looked at me and said nothing. We just looked at each other for the longest time. My heart was still. There wasn't anything to say or ask that would give more meaning to this moment.

The flight back to New York was largely uneventful. I spent a lot of time meditating. My mind tried to digest the past week's events. In recalling my time with Huzur, I knew that I had again sat face-to-face with a spiritual master and had my being realigned. I had peeked once again through a hole in reality. And now Dean . . . my old friend . . . and business partner . . . where was he going?

If there is a lesson to be learned from this journey, it is a lesson that every spiritual aspirant must learn. Hunker down in your spiritual practices and ask God to take your hand. Whatever you do, don't claim credit for it, just attribute it to God.

We are all headed into uncharted waters and a perfect storm is coming. Inshahallah (by God's will), may we be prepared.

www.ingramcontent.com/pod-product-compliance
Lightning Source LLC
Chambersburg PA
CBHW021144080526
44588CB00008B/202